A Guide to the Bars and Restaurants of *Breaking Bad* and *Better Call Saul*

A GUIDE TO

THE BARS AND RESTAURANTS OF

Breaking Bad and Better Call Saul

AIMEE MACPHERSON

UNIVERSITY OF NEW MEXICO PRESS | ALBUQUERQUE

Printed in the United States of America

ISBN 978-0-8263-6675-7 (paper)
ISBN 978-0-8263-6676-4 (ePub)

Library of Congress Control Number: 2024937278

Founded in 1889, the University of New Mexico sits on the traditional homelands of the Pueblo of Sandia. The original peoples of New Mexico—Pueblo, Navajo, and Apache—since time immemorial have deep connections to the land and have made significant contributions to the broader community statewide. We honor the land itself and those who remain stewards of this land throughout the generations and also acknowledge our committed relationship to Indigenous peoples. We gratefully recognize our history.

Cover photographs courtesy of Sony Pictures Television
Designed by Felicia Cedillos
Composed in Alegreya

CONTENTS

BETTER CALL SAUL

EL CAMINO: A BREAKING BAD MOVIE

FUNYUNS AND FINE WINE: HONORABLE MENTIONS OF FEATURED FLAVORS IN *BREAKING BAD* AND *BETTER CALL SAUL*

THAT'S A WRAP

588890
DOG HOUSE DRIVE IN INC.
1216 Central SW 505-243-1019
Albuquerque, New Mexico 87102
$

PREFACE

Albuquerque Offscreen

If you're reading this, odds are you're already familiar with *Breaking Bad* and *Better Call Saul*. The infamous characters from these two iconic series have dominated quality TV for over a decade. Combined, *Breaking Bad* and *Better Call Saul* is over a hundred hours of footage—watching just one series of either show is no short task. In addition to producing content that is watched and rewatched everywhere from South Korea to the Isle of Skye, the shows published a wealth of material like podcasts, YouTube videos, DVD extras, and webisodes. X (formerly Twitter) threads, Reddit AMA (Ask Me Anything) chats, and Instagram stories from cast and crew provide coverage of both the technical aspects of filming and the creative process of building these episodes. I haven't even listed the conventional interviews found on TV and in newspapers.

The detailed content provided by these shows about these shows are astounding. Researching, evaluating, and analyzing even a percentage of all this material is easily more than enough work for a doctoral degree. I'm sure there are many underway. That's before you enter the dizzying world of fans. Vince Gilligan, creator of *Breaking Bad*, even put out a book to celebrate the artists who pour so much into crafting images of their favorite TV characters.[1]

But what of Albuquerque, the fair city in which these dramas are set? The crystal meth and cucumber water are props; the sun-stained cars and crackling neon are the real deal. Each episode delicately

(*opposite page*) FIGURE 1. Dog House Drive In receipt, 2022. Courtesy of Aimee Macpherson.

drapes fiction over real restaurant booths and parking lots throughout the city—what locals affectionately refer to as "the 505"—as well the state. When you visit Albuquerque, you'll discover a whole new layer of detail to these beloved shows.

Albuquerque's heart is the Big I: a stack interchange between Interstate 25 and Interstate 40 made from towering pink concrete with a bright light-blue paint trim. Whichever road you pick here will take you all the way to the edge of the Americas: Mexico to Canada, California to New York. This is Walter White and Jimmy McGill's world, and we meet them both at a crossroads between good and bad. Even though we know what road Walt and Jimmy will eventually take, it doesn't ruin the drama or excitement of following them on their way. Walt's and Jimmy's fates are sealed in this dead-end sprawl of a city, littered with half-finished malls and baffling cul-de-sacs, a place where projects fall apart and cars, houses, and dreams are abandoned to bake in the relentless high-desert sun.

The city itself can seem like a crumbling autotopia, a forgotten temple to the American road trip, a footnote in the old songs of Route 66. The dated RVs, commercial trucks, and helmet-less bikers on our freeways only take the exit ramp to sleep, refuel the tank, or change a tire. They never mean to stay. The northern 505's neat 1950s suburbs are built to spec for an American dream nobody wants anymore: two cars in the garage, hot TV dinners and cold beer, a hot tub from a store permanently on closeout sale. Slippin' Jimmy shows us just how fragile those prefab dreams can be—instead of topping up the propane for his grill, he's sleeping in a cheesy nail salon, dreaming up his next big scheme.

Sure, Albuquerque's got farm-to-table dining, spas, single-origin espresso, and organic farms by the tractor load, but that's not why you're here. You're here to taste the bad, to wipe the sweat off your brow driving through the Big I in a beat-up rental. You want to ask yourself: Are you really that different from Saul? Would you have made a better choice than Pinkman? Given the chance to break bad like Walt, would you take it? Maybe you wish you had already.

So leave the fancy restaurants to New York, ignore the juicing in LA, forget your paleo diet bullshit, and come taste Albuquerque.

What's the worst that can happen? Scared you might like it? Or worse . . . you might want to stay?

Let Albuquerque be your theme park where the cowboys in Grandad's John Wayne movies have moved over for the slippery, manipulative characters of *Breaking Bad* and *Better Call Saul*. Savor the luscious portrayal of these small-screen giants as you step off the sofa to take in the hot sun, high altitude, and *la leche helada* of the Duke City.

Ordering a plate of enchiladas and a black coffee at one of these restaurants not only keeps your belly full but also keeps a unique cinematic history alive. Together, locals and international fans alike can continue to enjoy the hunting grounds of Walt, Jesse, and Gus, or raise a glass to Kim, Jimmy, and Howard. All it takes to participate is a drink or a meal at the real-deal bars and restaurants featured on these shows.

The world portrayed in *Breaking Bad* and *Better Call Saul* is not family friendly. Some of the locations portrayed in this show were selected because of their gritty appearance. Some were selected because they don't look gritty at all. All of them have regular patrons. Please use common sense when navigating the city, but also be conscientious of the regular customers who are just trying to enjoy a break at these local businesses.

NOTE

1. Vince Gilligan, *99.1% Pure: Breaking Bad Art* (San Rafael, CA: Insight Editions, 2021).

HOW TO USE THIS GUIDE

TWO SHOWS, SERVED THREE WAYS

The bars and restaurants in this book are organized by show, season, and episode. Skim through the following pages and you will see the locations are listed only once, in the order they first appear. For example, the Dog House Drive In is listed under *Breaking Bad*: Season 1. Of course, this takeout spot appears in *Breaking Bad* season 2 and *Better Call Saul* seasons 2 and 4. But the Dog House made its onscreen debut in *Breaking Bad* season 1. When you turn to the entry on the Dog House, you will see a list of episodes (with air dates) from both shows that featured this location after its debut. Structuring the book this way illustrates the evolution of the *Breaking Bad* and *Better Call Saul* universe, through its bars and restaurants, over space and time.

"Locations by Real Mealtimes" offers a more traditional guidebook feel, with entries divided into breakfast and lunch, lunch and dinner, small bites, and bars. The goal here is to help you find somewhere to eat or drink.

Finally, we have "Locations by Appearance in Both *Breaking Bad* and *Better Call Saul*." It only lists bars and restaurants that are featured in both shows (which you'll see abbreviated as *BB* and *BCS*, respectively, in location descriptions throughout the book). The goal here is to illustrate the unique way these two series feature repeat locations, sometimes revisiting them over decades of filming. It's also useful for visitors who are short on time, love both shows, and are quite hungry.

A WORD ON MENU PRICES

In this book, you will see $, $$, or $$$. These indicate a price bracket for main dishes on the menu, at the time of writing: $ means $5–$15, $$ means $15–$25, and $$$ means $30 and over. For bars and other purveyors, these designations apply to a single item—for example, a beer from Leo's Nightclub or a sweet treat from the Candy Lady. If you need to keep price points in check, please call the business in question for the most up-to-date information.

Breaking Bad

GARCIA'S KITCHEN

$

a.k.a. Garcia's Café
1736 Central Ave. SW, Albuquerque, 87104
(505) 842-0273
garbciaskitchen.com
Sunday–Saturday, 8:00 a.m.–3:00 p.m.

BB s1.e6, "Crazy Handful of Nothin'," March 2, 2008
BB s4.e4, "Bullet Points," August 7, 2011
BB s4.e5, "Shotgun," August 14, 2011

Garcia's Kitchen, along with the Dog House, is introduced into the *Breaking Bad* universe during a montage of Jesse Pinkman (Aaron Paul) dealing meth in "Crazy Handful of Nothin'." In real life, the two restaurants are just under ten minutes' walk apart on Central Avenue. Garcia's Kitchen has seven locations in Albuquerque; however, the location on Central is the only one that was featured in *Breaking Bad*. The restaurant later appears in a brief daytime time lapse in "Bullet Points," using a wide shot to anchor the restaurant's location on Central. It's not until the next episode, "Shotgun," that the restaurant exterior gets a longer feature, when Jesse collects Mike Ehrmantraut (Jonathan Banks) from the restaurant. He's just reversed the car down the alley to shake off Banger #1 (Anthony Martins), who's headed toward him on foot with a

FIGURE 2. Garcia's Kitchen exterior, *BB* s1.e6, "Crazy Handful of Nothin'" (2008). Courtesy of Sony Pictures Television.

shotgun hanging comfortably from his left hand. Banger #1 gets into his own vehicle (the one Jesse just slammed into) and drives off in pursuit of Jesse, leaving Mike in an empty alley watching the chase. "Honk once and I'll be in the parking lot," barks Mike into the phone as he walks underneath the Garcia's sign. At that moment, Jesse pulls up behind Mike. That means we don't get a scene inside, but you don't have to deny yourself the authentic New Mexican flavors of this eatery. Just remember that this Garcia's closes at 3:00 p.m.

Garcia's vintage neon sign at its Central Avenue location, complete with the blinking golden arrow pointing toward the restaurant, makes the place memorable. The neon sign is for "Garcia's Café," although the restaurant now goes by Garcia's Kitchen. The restaurant's exterior is decorated with intricate hand-painted murals; the inside is equally festive, with colorful *papeles picados* (Mexican garlands) and neat stacks of biscochitos in the display case on the counter. This restaurant is an Albuquerque institution, much like the Dog House. Andrew F. Garcia started the restaurant in 1975. Today Garcia's children run the seven locations around Albuquerque.[1] The kitchen continues to make all the classics—handmade corn and flour tortillas, *carne adovada*, menudo, salsa, and red and green chile, to name just a few examples. Breakfast is available anytime, just like the neon sign in the window says in "Shotgun."

On a cold winter day, there's nothing like a stew to heat you up. I love to get a pint of their green chile stew to go. It comes with a tortilla or sopapillas—usually, I go for a flour tortilla. This stew has a rich broth, and the signature flavor is a mild burn from the heat of roasted green chiles. It has a little bit of cubed potato and bite-size pieces of fried beef, and you can add pinto beans (a choice of whole or refried). Each spoonful delivers a tender, melt-in-your-mouth texture and a gentle warming spice. The kitchen also does a great menudo with hominy. This stew, also known as *mole de panza*, is made with tripe, or cow's stomach. It comes with a flour tortilla to help you soak up the broth, which is seasoned with red chile, hominy, lime, and onion.

Head to Garcia's on Central Avenue for a bowl of green chile stew. Save room for a couple of biscochitos.

DOG HOUSE DRIVE IN $

1216 Central Ave. SW, Albuquerque, 87102
(505) 243-1019
Monday–Saturday, 10:30 a.m.–9:00 p.m.

BB s1.e6, "Crazy Handful of Nothin'," March 2, 2008
BB s2.e1, "Seven Thirty-Seven," March 8, 2009
BCS s2.e8, "Fifi," April 4, 2016
BCS s4.e5, "Quite a Ride," September 3, 2018

The Dog House Drive In is hard to miss. This takeout joint is in a relatively small, one-story brick building in a parking lot that can hold at least ten vehicles. Above the black window grill is a large neon sign running the length of the building. It features a dachshund dog wagging its tail and biting into a blinking train of sausages. The word "DOG" is lit up in green while "HOUSE" is red, and the background is painted canary yellow. Under the words "DOG HOUSE" is the menu split into three panels, with items are printed in red with a chunky vintage typeface. Dachshunds have been at the center of hot dog culture going back a long, long time. According to the National Hot Dog and Sausage Council, there is some dispute about when ex-

FIGURE 3. Dog House Drive In exterior, *BCS* s4.e5, "Quite a Ride" (2018). Courtesy of Sony Pictures Television.

FIGURE 4. Dog House Drive In foot-long chili dog, 2022. Courtesy of Aimee Macpherson.

actly "dachshund," or "little-dog" sausage was created, but popular history credits it to 1487, in the city of Frankfurt, Germany.[2] By the 1890s, "hot dogs" were a commonplace snack at baseball games in North America. Albuquerque's Dog House opened in 1967 on Tenth Street and Central Avenue.[3] By 1969, it had moved a short way down the avenue to its current location on Twelfth and Central. Jimmie Hartley opened the restaurant in 1967, and at the time of writing, 2023, he still owns it. Originally from Texas, Hartley still eats at least one foot-long chili dog a week.[4]

In true drive-in fashion, you don't get out of your car to place your order, or eat it for that matter. Instead, a server comes to the window of your car. You make your selection from the oversized menu sign that hangs in front of the restaurant building. The inside of the Dog House is currently closed to customers, so you won't get a chance to see the Technicolor cinder blocks featured in the *Better Call Saul* episode "Quite a Ride." Outside, there are three sets of dining tables with bended plywood benches (a little different from the wooden benches depicted in the show), so you can sit outside like Jimmy McGill (Bob Odenkirk) and Kim Wexler (Rhea Seehorn) in

"Fifi." In this scene, both Kim and Jimmy are holding partially eaten hot dogs. They've brought beer with them, wrapped in brown paper bags. The Dog House does not serve beer.

If you want a hot dog like Kim and Jimmy, one that holds its shape without a paper wrapping, you'd probably have to go for a regular-size hot dog without any chili. But it's worth noting this fast-food eatery is known in Albuquerque for the foot-long hot dog. Unlike the short snacks on-camera, the foot-long is indeed 30.48 cm in length, making the dog somewhat droopy when you hold it. Add chili to the mix and the soft bun gets even softer. Leave it for a few seconds while you take a sip of soda and you'd be hard pressed to pick up the dog without the aid of the waxed paper its wrapped in. Until you've eaten around three-quarters of the entire foot, you really need to hold it with both hands to prevent the sausage from falling downward, which in turn lets gravity slide off most of the garnish.

When in Rome, order the foot-long chili dog. The chili is mild and the texture is curry-like. The flavor comes from ground spices like cumin and the texture from ground beef. The sauce here is not quite the Texan chili con carne, nor is it a deep-red New Mexican chile. This unique hybrid has an earthy orange color, which contrasts against the small cubes of diced white onion and the long, fluffy bun that cradles this dog. To round out the meal, order the tater tots. They are both crisp and tender and arrive in a little plastic-lined cardboard box. You'll also see Frito pie on the menu. If you haven't tried it by now, the Dog House is a good place to sample this iconic dish straight up, without any fussy embellishments. Lucy Herrman wrote an excellent piece in *Taos News* about Frito pie, hailing it as "one of New Mexico's most acclaimed comfort foods!"[5] It involves Frito corn chips topped with red chile con carne, cheese, and chopped onions, sometimes garnished with shredded lettuce and diced tomato. The Dog House serves it in a polystyrene takeout tray. Richard D. Dargan in the *Albuquerque Journal* says of the Dog House Frito pie that "some mixing is advised" to ensure all the chili covers the chips.[6]

Now let's take a closer look at the on-screen performance of this famous, beloved eatery. TV magic moment: the neon lights of the Dog House dachshund sign are rigged by the *Better Call Saul* lighting crew. A lighting technician is able to command how and when the neon flashed to control the look of the scene, right down to the dog's wagging tail.

Breaking Bad's "Crazy Handful of Nothin'" is the first time we see the Dog House Drive In, during a montage of Jesse selling meth. The idiom "in the doghouse" basically means being in a bad situation because someone is angry at you. There is something almost daring about the bold-as-brass symbolism of using the Dog House in *Breaking Bad* and *Better Call Saul*, a world where characters are frequently—if not constantly—in situations where someone is angry with them.[7] Like, super angry. Enraged.

Better Call Saul's "Quite a Ride" has loads of fun camera angles of the Dog House that echo how the eatery was shot in *Breaking Bad*'s "Crazy Handful of Nothin'." But it also has flair of its own. The parallel with *Saturday Night Fever* is downright funny. Instead of John Travolta with his double-decker pizza and heeled shoes, we have the somewhat more stressed-looking Jimmy strutting along in his sneakers, coaxing himself into hustler mode as Saul Goodman. Again "in the doghouse" serves as a kind of fatalistic mark on both Jesse and Jimmy when they are at Dog House. They will both be in their respective "doghouses" soon enough, but for a moment, the hot dogs are sizzling and the going is good.

This fast-food restaurant is an institution. It works as both a piece of irony for an international audience and as a straight-up eatery where anyone, from fancy downtown lawyers to moody teenagers, can stop for a bite. For a full Dog House experience, I recommend going at night. If you time your visit with the New Mexican monsoon season (July–September), you may be lucky enough to experience the wet tarmac and puddles reflecting the neon signage, as seen in "Quite a Ride." It doesn't rain very often in New Mexico, so on set the look was achieved through a historic trick of the trade called "wet downs," in which a large quantity of water is brought to set by a hose truck. The special effects department coordinates with the transportation department to hose down the scene just before filming to get that tarmac glistening on-camera.

Get a foot-long chili cheese hot dog, plus tater tots. Eat with the window down so your car doesn't smell of chili dog for the rest of the night. Round out the meal with a soda fountain Pepsi.

JAVA JOE'S $

a.k.a. Tuco Salamanca's HQ
906 Park Ave. SW., Ste. 3045, Albuquerque, 87102
(505) 765-1514
downtownjavajoes.com
Sunday–Saturday, 6:30 a.m.–3:30 p.m.

BB s1.e6, "Crazy Handful of Nothin'," March 2, 2008

Java Joe's appears just once in *Breaking Bad*'s universe. But once you've seen the on-screen drama, this location is unforgettable. In real life, this café and artisan coffee shop is unpretentious and welcoming, totally unlike Tuco Salamanca (Raymond Cruz), the villain whose HQ exterior was filmed here. As a fan of the show, you may decide to go there just for the mural on the east outdoor wall of the building rather than their delicious roasted-in-house coffee, but please don't take a picture without being a patron of the business. If you're dining in, you can't go wrong with a "bottomless mug" of

FIGURE 5. Java Joe's exterior, showing us the explosion from the fulminated mercury that "Heisenberg" smashes on the ground in Tuco's HQ, BB s1.e6, "Crazy Handful of Nothin'" (2008). Courtesy of Sony Pictures Television. Figure 5. Java Joe's exterior, showing us the explosion from the fulminated mercury that "Heisenberg" smashes on the ground in Tuco's HQ, *BB* s1.e6, "Crazy Handful of Nothin'" (2008). Courtesy of Sony Pictures Television.

FIGURE 6. Java Joe's enchiladas, 2022. Courtesy of Aimee Macpherson.

drip coffee. The menu offers specialty drinks, including a Grasshopper coffee, which gets its minty dark-chocolate flavor from crème de menthe and crème de cacao syrups. A yogurt parfait with housemade granola will set you up for a great morning.

I got to Java Joe's in time for an earlyish lunch. The cashier recommended breakfast enchiladas: three corn tortillas layered with cheddar cheese, black beans, and eggs, smothered in your choice of chile. I had my eggs over easy, with Christmas-style chile (both red and green chile on the same dish). It was like getting a warm hug from an old friend. The made-from-scratch food feels hearty without sending you into a sleep-isode. Tender beans, bright-yellow egg yolks, and homemade tortillas really make the dish sing. The chile delivered a lot of flavor without overpowering. They serve the meal stacked on two hot ceramic plates that are just out of the oven, keeping the meal warm and inviting you to take your time. My table looked out on to Park Avenue, framed by several pots of pink geraniums. A couple of diners next to me enjoyed a table all to themselves with a hot breakfast and a book. I even bumped into Java Joe's co-owner Michael Phlieger, who was seated, like many of his customers, at a table with his iPad, taking a call.

Phlieger was kind enough to stop and talk to me about the book and his experience of owning a local café that now has a world-famous exterior. Phlieger's food philosophy is "keep it simple." The eatery values keeping their food affordable, and they try to avoid serving food that comes preprepared, which means homemade food sourced from the farmers' market—nothing out of a bag or a box. The café also features eclectic local art and coffee beans available for purchase by the pound. Phlieger's philosophy and the inviting interior has served the business well for over twenty-five years, attracting locals year-round.

The restaurant is also no stranger to film crews. Phlieger mentioned that the funny thing about TV shooting is the length of time between the day of filming and the air date of the episode that features your location. Your friends give you an excited call when they see your business on TV, but for the business owner, all the action happened months and months ago. The air date is just a regular day at the shop.

The interior of the café does not, of course, resemble Tuco's headquarters, but—subject to availability—they sell "Tuco's Hideaway" T-shirts with an illustration of Walt outside the business. Their mugs featuring Java Joe's old-school logo are the gift you should snag for a friend back home.

"Crazy Handful of Nothin'" is a landmark episode for so many reasons. Perhaps the most obvious one is that this is the first time we hear Walt (Bryan Cranston) refer to himself as Heisenberg, a reference to the German chemist famous for his pioneering work on quantum mechanics and who, like Walt, also had terminal cancer.[8] When Walt blows up Tuco's hideout, we get a flavor of the ultraviolence that makes this show famous. Walt doesn't do eye for an eye; instead, he escalates, tapping into his newfound villainous capacity for creative aggression.

Order the filter coffee and breakfast enchiladas. Sit back and enjoy the ambience.

NOTES

1. Garcia's Kitchen, "Our History," accessed September 10, 2022, https://www.garciaskitchen.com/our-history/.

2. National Hot Dog and Sausage Council, "Hot Dog History," accessed January 26, 2024, http://hot-dog.org/culture/hot-dog-history.

3. Better Business Bureau, "Business Profile: Dog House Drive Inn [*sic*]," accessed March 8, 2023, https://www.bbb.org/us/nm/albuquerque/profile/carry-out-food/dog-house-drive-inn-0806-17693.

4. Jozelyn Escobedo, "Inside the 505: Story Behind the Iconic Dog House," KOAT News, updated February 22, 2019, https://www.koat.com/article/inside-the-505-story-behind-the-iconic-dog-house/26458038.

5. Lucy Herrman, "Frito Pie: A Classic New Mexico Comfort Food," *Taos News*, June 23, 2021, https://www.taosnews.com/la-vida/food-and-drink/frito-pie-a-classic-new-mexico-comfort-food/article_9c14a06f-34b8-5a45-b046-396654b6b81d.html.

6. Richard S. Dargan, "Dog House Remains Iconic with Its Hot Dogs, Burgers and Shakes," *Albuquerque Journal*, January 4, 2023.

7. *Merriam-Webster*, s.v. "in the doghouse (*idiom*)," updated November 27, 2023, https://www.merriam-webster.com/dictionary/in%20the%20doghouse.

8. Wikipedia, s.v. "Werner Heisenberg," last modified January 20, 2024, 06:30, https://en.wikipedia.org/wiki/Werner_Heisenberg.

TACO SAL

$

9621 Menaul Blvd. NE, Albuquerque, 87112
(505) 298-2210
facebook.com/p/Taco-Sal-100054574864886
Monday–Saturday, 11:00 a.m.–8:00 p.m.

BB s2.e2, "Grilled," March 15, 2009
BB s2.e10, "Over," May 10, 2009
BB s3.e11, "Abiquiu," May 30, 2010

According to their sign outside, Taco Sal has been in business since 1960. The sign, with a pale-pink background and hand-painted roadrunners framing the white lettering, turns into glorious red neon at night. The vintage good looks of the exterior are reason enough to drop in on this restaurant. But Taco Sal also offers plenty of New Mexican classics, including tacos, stuffed sopapillas, huevos rancheros, carne adovada, burritos, and chips and salsa.

The location appears several times in *Breaking Bad*, and the show makes good use of the restaurant's wide windows and its excellent neon. Taco Sal is the local eatery where Skyler White (Anna Gunn)

FIGURE 7. Taco Sal exterior, 2022. Courtesy of Aimee Macpherson.

FIGURE 8. Taco Sal's hard-shell tacos, 2022. Courtesy of Aimee Macpherson.

and her sister Marie Schrader (Betsy Brandt) hand out homemade "missing" signs for Walt. At the end of season 2, Walt meets Jesse at Taco Sal and announces his decision to retire from making meth (ha!). Subsequent episodes reveal that decision was short lived.

Taco Sal is also featured in a more tender moment of *Breaking Bad* season 3. Jesse has dinner with Andrea Cantillo (Emily Rios) and her son, Brock Cantillo (Ian Posada), at the eatery. He does a few goofy tricks to keep Brock amused and we get a good shot of Brock's hard-shell tacos. It's an all-too-fleeting, wholesome, unremarkable moment for a couple who are doomed to failure, violence, and pain. The poignancy of this lost relationship runs with Jesse all the way to *El Camino: A* Breaking Bad *Movie*, where we see a photo of Andrea and her son in the background when Jesse gets a beating at the compound of "Uncle Jack" Welker (Michael Bowen).

Taco Sal is in a shopping center in Albuquerque's Northeast Heights, next to a business called Comic Warehouse. Across the street is a Mister Car Wash, formerly known as Octopus Car Wash, the location of Walt's "legit" business—i.e., money-laundering hub. (Learn more about this car wash in the "Vending Machines" chapter.)

In *Breaking Bad*, Taco Sal's dining tables are in the front of the restaurant, framed by the decorative windows and vintage signage. You step in through the same door you see in the show, but when I visited, the front space was cleared, tables and chairs stacked against the wall. Ahead is the semi-open kitchen, and a doorway to your right will take you to the current seating area. It has brownish vinyl dining booths with painted murals of mountains on the walls. At the front of the room by the windows are tables covered in Mexican oilcloths printed with colorful illustrations of flowers like hibiscuses and chrysanthemums.

I visited Taco Sal for an early lunch. There were already several booths taken. My table was close to the window, and I ordered the Tres Tacos dinner plate, which gave me three hard-shell beef tacos, in an homage to Brock. The *salsa roja* at Taco Sal is brought to you when you take a seat, no questions asked. Flavorful and mild, it comes in a little bowl with a plastic basket of corn chips. My tacos were garnished with shredded iceberg lettuce, grated jack cheese, and diced tomato. Inside was lightly seasoned warm ground beef. The dinner plate came with Spanish rice, refried beans, and a sopapilla. Everything was made to order and hot from the stovetop.

Taco Sal has a local and vocal following. One diner greeted his dinner plate by exclaiming, "Honey, call the doctor!" It looked like he had ordered the Brunch Sopapilla: a puffy square of sopapilla dough stuffed with beans and carne adovada, smothered in red chile, and topped with shredded cheese plus two fried eggs. Refried beans and *papitas* managed to fit on the side of the plate. Another patron leaned over their table, pointed to my tacos, and said, "How'd you like that?" Outside, a third customer leaned out of the open window of his car and asked, "You enjoy your lunch? Pretty good, right?" He didn't wait for an answer before pulling out of the parking lot, because he knew his assertions were correct. Taco Sal is certainly a good lunch spot.

Stick to the *Breaking Bad* theme by ordering order the Tres Tacos dinner plate. If you're looking for something a bit more filling, the Brunch Sopapilla is a great place to start.

BURT'S TIKI LOUNGE

Permanently closed
313 Gold Ave. SW, Albuquerque, 87102
515 Central Ave. NW, Albuquerque, 87102

BB s2.e5, "Breakage," April 5, 2009
BCS s3.e6, "Off Brand," May 15, 2017

Breaking Bad and *Better Call Saul* both feature Burt's Tiki Lounge once. We only see the exterior on the show, so I am not going to discuss tiki bars and their midcentury rise to popularity in suburban America, or the complex defining visual features of these bars, with their romanticization of Polynesian and other tropical cultures. Burt's was known for being very good at selling drinks that were far too strong and playing music that was far too loud. You couldn't hear yourself think, and that was exactly why you went.

In *Breaking Bad*, Christian "Combo" Ortega (Rodney Rush) deals drugs to two girls in a car outside the bar, and in *Better Call Saul*, Chuck McGill (Michael McKean) walks past the bar on his way to a pay phone. Both shows feature characters outside the same Burt's sign, but the sign appears on different streets. Burt's was established

FIGURE 9. Burt's Tiki Lounge exterior, *BB* s2.e5, "Breakage" (2009). Courtesy of Sony Pictures Television.

in 1999 on Gold Avenue, which is where the *Breaking Bad* scene was shot. In 2016, the bar moved to Central Avenue and took the sign with it—this is where the *Better Call Saul* scene was shot. Burt's Tiki Lounge is now permanently closed, and the sign has disappeared from Central Avenue. Its latest location is currently occupied by a nightclub called Cake. The last I could find on the whereabouts of the sign was a blog from 2019 noting the sign was listed on Craigslist for free.[1] Answers on a postcard please!

Since the cameras don't go inside the bar, the sign performs on-screen as a film-set facade. In emphasizing the embellished exterior signage, and not the functioning bar behind it, the shows reimagine real Albuquerque streets as a neo-Western setting. Burt's signage replaces the Western saloon, and cracked tarmac replaces the dirt road. Western false fronts have a long tradition in the America West outside of their role on camera. They were used in the 1800s to make pop-up makeshift wooden buildings look more impressive to potential customers.[2] It's more likely than not that Albuquerque had many of these storefronts during this era. But it's not just the architecture of a "false front" that creates symbolism and meaning in the cityscape of *Breaking Bad* and *Better Call Saul*. The phrase "false front" can be used to describe behavior that is "intended to deceive"[3]—a running theme for the protagonists in this TV world.

It's worth noting that both Combo and Chuck are filmed outside the bar at night, on foot, a pedestrian reprieve from an auto-centric show set in an auto-centric city. If you visit the two locations for Burt's featured in the shows, please get out of the car and walk around on foot. Go at night. Look upward at the signage for dead and long-gone stores. Then find a nice cocktail downtown and rejoin the land of the living.

While Burt's is closed for business and the sign is gone, still open in the neighborhood are Bar Uno and Carrie's, both of which were featured on *Better Call Saul*.

SAVOY BAR & GRILL $$$

a.k.a. bar in Omaha
10601 Montgomery Blvd. NE, Albuquerque, 87111
(505) 294-9463
savoyabq.com
Wednesday–Sunday, 3:00 p.m.–9:00 p.m.

BB s2.e6, "Peekaboo," April 12, 2009
BCS s6.e11, "Breaking Bad," August 1, 2022

At the real-life Savoy Bar & Grill, you're more likely to encounter Albuquerque's professional class of doctors, lawyers, and scientists than Skinny Pete (Charles Baker) and company. It will clash horribly with your pursuit of a sinister drug-dealing underworld in a city that has fallen on hard times. Spoiler alert: Albuquerque has great farmers' markets! But if you can put that disappointment aside, by all means head out to Savoy for a delightful, unpretentious, locally sourced meal. The restaurant boasts "classic and contemporary California Wine Country in the Northeast Heights."[4] I'd say this is

FIGURE 10. Savoy Bar & Grill interior, as a bar in Omaha, where Gene (under the alias Viktor) is working his scam victim Alfred, *BCS* s6.e11, "Breaking Bad" (2022). Courtesy of Sony Pictures Television.

an accurate portrayal of the menu and vibe. It's everything Walt couldn't afford before he started cooking meth.

The broiled double-boned pork chop is a long-standing classic and perfect for dinner. It comes with an abundance of sides, including bacon farro pilaf, heritage greens, shaved fennel, grilled plums, allium vinaigrette, and blackberry gastrique. The sugary-sour syrup of the gastrique really sets off the meal both in terms of flavor and color on the plate. If you want to relax al fresco, the patio lounge menu has plenty of fun options for something lighter, including plenty of indulgent, flavorful appetizers and salads. You can scale up to an oak-fired goat cheese with a Parma prosciutto crisp, or keep it simple with soup and salad, depending on your preference.

The appetite for an unsavory Albuquerque celebrated by fans of *Breaking Bad* and *Better Call Saul* causes much ire to some of its more well-heeled locals. As local Ann Abel opines in *Forbes* magazine, "I got a new appreciation of my hometown. And I almost forgot, for a few hours, that *Breaking Bad* also took place here."[5] The squalor of a faded Route 66 Americana is what people visiting Albuquerque for *Breaking Bad* so often crave. At Savoy, however, Frasier and Niles Crane would be perfectly comfortable with the wine menu. Enjoy happy hour from 4:00 p.m. to 6:00 p.m. daily. They offer a rotation of small plates to go with your beverage of choice, which is a great way to sample the menu if you don't want to go all out on fine dining. There is outdoor seating if the weather is agreeable, but for the sake of our homage to *Breaking Bad* you will have to sit inside.

Although this restaurant appears just once in *Breaking Bad*, it provides the location for a real knockout scene in the episode "Peekaboo"—please follow Walt in aggressively whispering "Fuck you!" so as not to disturb your fellow diners when you re-create the iconic moment. There probably won't be jazz piano in the background while you do it, but I think you can manage. Walt's encounter with Gretchen Schwartz (Jessica Hecht) at Savoy delightfully encapsulates the disconnect between his new shoot-from-the-hip livelihood and the restraint of a professional class that rejected him, symbolized by Gretchen. This restaurant signifies "upscale." It's not a place where you expect to be told you ruined someone's life—especially when all you're trying to do is call them out on a lie. Walt's confrontation with Gretchen comes after he reveals he's been lying to his wife about the payment of his medical bills. He told Skyler that Gretchen was paying them, and while she did indeed offer to pay them, Walt turned down the offer.

Walt's cover is falling apart, but he's barely able to uphold a patina of courtesy. When explaining himself to Gretchen, his tone is irreverent, snarky and angry: "I don't owe you an explanation; I owe you an apology, and I have apologized." But, of course, this display doesn't stick with Gretchen. She isn't a skittish drug dealer; she's a wealthy, sober woman. Walt's failed attempt to parley in the language of a professional class he has already left speaks volumes. It seems like the last grasp he has on this polite world is the way he shouts in a whisper so as not to cause a scene. His behavior and tenor is inappropriate for both the restaurant setting and the emotional situation before him. It would be more appropriate, say, when he's bullying Jesse in a beat-up RV. Gretchen tells him, "This isn't you," which pretty much hits the nail on the head. Walt as thug has arrived! He goes further to the true root of his rage—she made her money off his work. If she hadn't cut him out, he wouldn't have been in need of her charity. Tellingly, neither have food or drink in front of them, the bare plates emphasizing the awkwardness and discomfort they both experience. This is not a moment where the two characters are going to break bread.

Savoy is used as a location in *Better Call Saul*, almost at the end of season 6 in episode 11, titled "Breaking Bad." This time, we are at the long, glossy black stone bar top with Gene Takovic (Jimmy's new identity after relocating to Omaha, Nebraska). While Savoy doesn't have a Rusty Nail on the menu, you can choose from plenty of craft cocktails. I recommend the Blue Bear. It's got local gin, simple syrup, lime juice, blackberries, mint, and rhubarb bitters. It looks elegant but avoids being overly sweet. (I reckon the mother bear in *Blueberries for Sal* would love it.) As for the scene at the bar, Gene calls himself Viktor, in homage to his scams with Kim in season 2. "Viktor" endures a karaoke song, buying a drink for Alfred Hawthorne Hill (Devin Ratray) and losing money on bets we are pretty sure Jimmy knows how to handle. What's the game here? Well, sure enough, Viktor leaves with the upper hand: He's spiked Alfred's drink with barbiturates and sank his own drink down a tube to a hot water bottle hidden in his jacket. The guy is stone-cold sober and ready to execute a high-stakes scam. Dastardly and corrupt, Viktor reminds us that maybe Chuck McGill had a point when he ranted about his brother, "What a sick joke" (s3.e5, "Chicanery").

Head to the bar for a cocktail like Viktor, or sit in the dining room for a white tablecloth like Walt. Happy hour is a good place to start: Wednesday–Sunday, 3:00 p.m.–6:00 p.m.

THE BOURBON HOUSE $$

a.k.a. Saul Goodman & Associates
9800 Montgomery Blvd. NE, Ste. 3, Albuquerque, 87111
(505) 481-9948
bourbonhouseabq.com
Sunday, 11:00 a.m.–8:00 p.m.
Tuesday–Wednesday, 11:00 a.m.–10:00 p.m.
Thursday–Saturday, 11:00 a.m.–2:00 a.m.

BB s2.e8, "Better Call Saul," April 26, 2009
BB s2.e9, "4 Days Out," May 3, 2009
BB s2.e11, "Mandala," May 17, 2009
BB s2.e12, "Phoenix," May 24, 2009
BB s3.e2, "Caballo sin Nombre," March 28, 2010
BB s3.e4, "Green Light," April 11, 2010
BB s3.e5, "Más," April 18, 2010
BB s3.e13, "Full Measure," June 13, 2010
BB s4.e1, "Box Cutter," July 17, 2011
BB s4.e4, "Bullet Points," August 7, 2011
BB s5.e1, "Live Free or Die," July 15, 2012
BB s5.e2, "Madrigal," July 22, 2012

FIGURE 11. Bourbon House, as Saul Goodman's office exterior, *BB* s2.e8, "Better Call Saul" (2009). Courtesy of Sony Pictures Television.

FIGURE 12. Bourbon House exterior, 2022. Courtesy of Aimee Macpherson.

BB s5.e7, "Say My Name," August 26, 2012
BCS s4.e5, "Quite a Ride," September 3, 2018
BCS s6.e4, "Hit and Run," May 2, 2022
BCS s6.e5, "Black and Blue," May 9, 2022
BCS s6.e9, "Fun and Games," May 16, 2022
BCS s6.e12, "Waterworks," August 8, 2022
El Camino, October 11, 2019

This place is a cornerstone of the *Breaking Bad* and *Better Call Saul* universe, if not *the* location that bridges the gap between the two shows. For many years, this address housed a shuttered business, but I'm very happy to report that a new bar opened in 2022. The neighboring location, the Dirty Bourbon, a wildly popular "Old Western Style Saloon and Dance Hall,"[6] purchased the property and launched the Bourbon House. The Dirty Bourbon has long been a favorite of city revelers and country dancers alike but has never provided food. Now hot meals plus "over 100 bourbons" are available next door at the Bourbon House, starting when doors open at 11:00 a.m. It also means you can get inside the building that provided the exterior location for Saul Goodman & Associates during *Breaking Bad* and the interior in *Better Call Saul*'s final season. The patio at the front of the building was remodeled, and it now features a raised concrete patio, low ironwork fencing, and sunshade arrangements.

The bar, as advertised, has an overwhelming variety of bourbons to select, and drinks are poured by a knowledgeable staff. Their menu has a variety of sandwiches, appetizers, and salads, and pizzas suitable for soaking up hard liquor but tasty enough to enjoy on their own. It's the desserts that really stole my heart at this restaurant. The Caramel Filled Churros are served with smoked maple-and-bourbon praline ice cream, fresh berries, and drizzles of chocolate and caramel. Welcome to flavor country.

When I visited in late spring, there were pink petunias in hanging baskets, making the exterior remarkably different from its on-screen look in *Breaking Bad* and *Better Call Saul*. The two front window panels now open for a seamless transition between the inside and the outside of the bar during sunny weather. The front door and panel next to it still have a shiny patina. Looking out from the bar patio, the view is largely unchanged: a parking lot in the foreground and, behind the pickups, SUVs, and hatchbacks, a gas station, a pet store called Long Leash On Life, and a PurLife Dispensary.

We first see the exterior of Saul's office in season 2, episode 8 of *Breaking Bad*, appropriately titled "Better Call Saul." Walt scoffs at Saul's credentials when he sees the firm's cheesy storefront in an unassuming strip mall, an inflatable statue of liberty looming down from the rooftop. But Jesse reminds him, and us the viewers snug at home, that this is exactly who they need for the job: "You don't want a criminal lawyer; you want a *criminal* lawyer." It's easy to forget that Saul has an excellent reputation among his clients. It's just that those clients aren't exactly respectable . . . or law abiding. And what's so clever about the location of his law office and his bombastic persona is that it appeals to his prospective clients, not your regular suburban dad. The notion that this look is off-putting to everyone else really doesn't matter to Saul—he's not trying to get in their good graces anyway. For this go-round, the joke is on Walt.

Saul has something Walt needs, that he can't cook up in the back of an RV: a license to practice law in New Mexico.

The Montgomery location of Saul's office does not leave us with many traces of the set we experience on-screen. In *Breaking Bad*, the interior of Saul's office is a set. The unmistakable interior decor, with the constitution inscribed behind Saul's desk, framed by Ionic columns, could be broken down and stored away. The interior of the Montgomery location was featured in the final season of *Better Call Saul*. The first glimpse inside showed us a room empty save for a ceramic toilet. Jimmy invites Francesca Liddy (Tina Parker), his legal secretary at Wexler McGill, to resume her job with him at his new firm, Saul Goodman & Associates. Francesca agrees to take on the job of legal secretary to "Saul Goodman" on one condition: she decorates the office. Francesca's panache for interior decoration is the on-screen reason why Saul was blessed with a striking office. The wallpaper printed with the constitution, that grand desk, and the billiard room lighting was all her doing. Today Francesca's decor is no longer in evidence at the Montgomery location, but you can sit in your car outside and recite Jesse's infamous line about *criminal* lawyers.

Just to make the psychogeography of your visit a bit more complicated, *El Camino* features Duke City Sports Bar as the business that replaces Saul's law office once it shutters for good. The sports bar was a real Albuquerque business that once operated at that location. It's only visible for a moment, during one of Vince Gilligan's signature time-lapse pieces, but the framing looks like a nod to those high, wide establishing shots of Saul Goodman & Associates. This makes it something of an "Easter egg" for the avid fans of *Breaking Bad* and *Better Call Saul*, but it's also an example of how the showrunners use a location for decades of filming. Storefronts change, businesses close. A shuttered business finally reopening as the Bourbon House is a completely unremarkable event in the real world of Albuquerque. In the universe of our beloved shows, an office for a *criminal* lawyer being replaced by Duke City Sports Bar changes the emotional landscape. *El Camino* recaptures the new look of this strip mall and puts it right back into the world of these characters by including a shot of the new bar. It's a tongue-in-cheek nod to the continuity sticklers—yes, of course it doesn't look the same as it did in *Breaking Bad*. But rather than fight it, *El Camino* turns the changed landscape of the strip mall into a visual commentary on the finality of Saul's business practice closing. Saul's done. The office is now a bar. Get over it . . .

Visiting an unremarkable, neglected strip mall can be a way to counter the myopic vision of the place. In many ways, both shows absolutely agree with the values of the society of the spectacle: "Everything that was directly experienced has been replaced with its representation in the form of images."[7] The whole city is a set. By going to hang out in this corner of the earth, you're choosing to explore what it's like to enjoy being in an environment you've been warned against. You've likely been told there is "nothing to see here," but by inhabiting the space for yourself, you can see value and beauty where it's traditionally been missed. At a glance, 9800 Montgomery NE may just look like a sunblasted concrete corner of the earth, but the emotional markers of the show make the real-life weeds peeping through the cracked asphalt mean so much more.

Head to the Bourbon House and tuck into something hearty. Order a nine-year-old Knob Creek bourbon, straight up, in homage to Hank. If the spirit moves you, head next door and sample the Dirty Bourbon's 1,300-square-foot dance floor, complete with a mechanical bull.

TWISTERS BURGERS AND BURRITOS $

a.k.a. Los Pollos Hermanos
4275 Isleta Blvd. SW, Albuquerque, 87105
(505) 822-2727
mytwisters.com/restaurants/isleta
Sunday–Saturday, 6:00 a.m.–8:00 p.m.

BB s2.e11, "Mandala," May 17, 2009
BB s2.e12, "Phoenix," May 24, 2009
BB s3.e1, "No Más," March 21, 2010
BB s3.e5, "Más," April 18, 2010
BB s3.e6, "Sunset," April 25, 2010
BB s3.e8, "I See You," May 9, 2010
BB s4.e5, "Shotgun," August 14, 2011
BB s4.e7, "Problem Dog," August 28, 2011
BB s4.e8, "Hermanos," September 4, 2011
BB s4.e9, "Bug," September 11, 2011
BB s5.e1, "Live Free or Die," July 15, 2012
BCS s3.e2, "Witness," April 17, 2017
BCS s3.e4, "Sabrosito," May 1, 2017
BCS s3.e8, "Slip," June 5, 2017
BCS s4.e2, "Breathe," August 13, 2018
BCS s4.e4, "Talk," August 27, 2018
BCS s4.e9, "Wiedersehen," October 1, 2018
BCS s5.e4, "Namaste," March 9, 2020
BCS s6.e5, "Black and Blue," May 9, 2022
BCS s6.e8, "Point and Shoot," July 11, 2022
El Camino, October 11, 2019

The location for Gustavo (Gus) Fring's Los Pollos Hermanos is a Twisters on Isleta (Spanish for "little island") Boulevard in the South Valley, just outside Albuquerque's city limits. It's very near Isleta Pueblo, home to Tiwa-speaking Native Americans and one of the larger nineteen pueblos in New Mexico. Isleta Pueblo was established in the 1300s, and Hispanic farmers have been farming land with irrigated water from the Rio Grande since colonization. Some

FIGURE 13. Los Pollos Hermanos (shot at Twisters Burgers and Burritos) curly fry debut, *BB* s2.e11, "Mandala" (2009). Courtesy of Sony Pictures Television.

FIGURE 14. Twisters curly fries, 2022. Courtesy of Aimee Macpherson.

of the adobe homes in this area are four hundred years old. This part of Isleta Boulevard is close to El Camino de Real Tierra Adentro, a historic trade route over one thousand miles long that connects Mexico City to Ohkay Owingeh, one of New Mexico's Tewa-speaking pueblos whose homeland is just north of Santa Fe.[8]

By contrast, Los Pollos Hermanos is a fast-food joint that serves as a front for the drug smuggling operation of Gus Fring (Giancarlo Esposito), a place where weary travelers can find fried chicken sandwiches or a drug kingpin. *Breaking Bad* and *Better Call Saul* have invested the humble Twisters restaurant with a mythical significance and an eerie presence in this quiet rural community. It's also created an on-screen restaurant that is physically different from the original location. In season 3, episode 1 of *Better Call Saul*, "No Más," cartel captain Hector Salamanca (Mark Margolis) visits Gus in a rage, after cops raid his *paletería*, El Griego Guiñador. He is quickly ushered into Gus's office at Los Pollos so they can talk crime. The set for Gus's office goes back to *Breaking Bad*. "Sabrosito," in season 3 of *Better Call Saul*, is the episode that first uses actor action to travel from the real restaurant location (Twisters) to the restaurant office (built onstage) in one continuous plot point. This office doesn't exist at the Twisters location, but it does on-screen at Los Pollos Hermanos. The shot sequence had to be contrived in such a way as to make the audience believe both the set and location were in the same place. In this regard, Gus's office is much like Saul's office at the nail salon: a fictional stage that uses the geography of a real location to ground it.

The Los Pollos menu makes many appearances in both *Breaking Bad* and *Better Call Saul*. The scripts are very specific about what the characters order at this famous eatery. In the *Better Call Saul* episode "Witness," Jimmy orders a Pollos Classic with coffee for $3.19, no to the extra salsa but yes to ketchup. Jimmy tracks a courier for Mike in *Better Call Saul* season 3, episode 2, "Witness," and reports that the courier orders a number 3 with potatoes and coffee—"bold," with the extra salsa—and pays with cash.

Twisters does have a number 3 on the menu (it's a New Mexico burrito with egg, potato, green chile, and cheese). The food offered at Gus's eatery is different from the real-life food at Twisters, with one caveat: on the actual Twisters menu at Isleta, you can get several chicken dishes. Two that stood out for me were the Scorpion Ranch chicken sandwich (the Classic comes with pickles and sauce, the Ultimate adds bacon, lettuce, and tomato) and the crispy boneless wings, which can be slathered in your choice of three sauces: Mild Buffalo, Garlic Parmesan, and Honey Chipotle BBQ. Order them Naked to go sauce free.

When I walked into the restaurant, the woman at the counter (the staff use an iPad these days instead of the old-school cash till featured on the show), sported a yellow Los Pollos Hermanos apron. A priest was the only other diner, sitting down for a breakfast burrito and taking a long phone call, a paper napkin tucked into his Roman collar. A steady stream of drive-through orders kept the staff busy.

I kept it simple and ordered curly fries from the favorites menu, then sat down in one of the booths, basking in the functional design and poppy graphics. I didn't sit in Walt's booth because too much sun was hitting the window. My fries came in a logo-embossed white polystyrene box. The Twisters curly fries are cut from whole potatoes, using what is essentially an industrial-sized spiralizer. This happens off-site. Fried in hot oil, they are served straight up with salt. This provides the perfect base for their famous Chile Cheese Fries, which serves the fries under an assortment of bold sauces: Green Chile Queso, Garnish, Ranch Drizzle, Guac, and a side of Scorpion. They are vegetarian.

Remember the drinks fountain where Jimmy overfills the sugar in his coffee when he spies Hector paying the restaurant a visit in "Sabrosito"? That's a recessed counter now filled with *Breaking Bad* photos and memorabilia. The counter itself has a letter organizer full of handwritten notes left at the restaurant by visiting fans. The trash can used by Saul and Gus in Gus's first appearance on *Better Call Saul* ("Witness") has moved locations and is now by the ordering counter. Twisters does serve fountain drinks, but the fountain at this location is behind the serving counter. Like Blake's, they offer Pepsi, not Coca-Cola.

A New Mexican favorite you might order at Twisters is the breakfast burrito. Twisters recommends the South Valley burrito (number 5 on the menu) which comes with chorizo, egg, potatoes, red chile, and cheese wrapped in a flour tortilla. It's an appropriate choice since this Twisters is located in the South Valley. Humble and functional, the breakfast burrito is an efficient way to eat your first meal of the day—no utensils required. On the go, it's traditionally eaten with one hand while the other guides a Dodge pickup along the interstate. You can sit down to eat it with a knife and fork, so long as you smother it in chile: red, green, or both ("Christmas" if you're trying to pass as a local). This breakfast of champions comes in all sorts of combinations and accidentally caters to many different modern diets—vegans (the bean burrito), vegetarians (the egg and chile burrito), and meat lovers (carne adovada, sausage, or that old friend, bacon). The gluten-free among us could probably order the burrito—hold the flour tortilla—but why don't you order huevos rancheros with corn tortillas instead?

It's worth taking a moment to enjoy the restaurant's particularly unlovely parking lot. Think back on your favorite establishing shots of the fast-food chain, or maybe pull up a scene on your phone while you're standing there with the traffic thundering past and the sun beating down on you and your car. My favorite is the reveal of the restaurant in *Better Call Saul*'s "Witness." Try and frame the shot yourself with your fingers and you'll come to a whole new level of appreciation for the on-screen look of this famous fast-food chain. The cinematography of this Twisters parking lot is the definition of how to reframe the ugly, the overlooked, and the commonplace into a fabulous and dramatically tense back drop for some of the best TV drama ever. Sidenote: between Twisters and its neighboring store Quality Baits & Pond Fish is a grassy paddock. During filming, an angry emu was living there. Last time I was there, the emu had gone, but be sure to check if he's in residence when you visit!

After eating my curly fries, I walked out to the parking lot. There I met a young man called Shishir and his father, traveling from Massachusetts. They were on a coast-to-coast road trip for the summer, stopping in Albuquerque to visit a few sites from their favorite shows, *Breaking Bad* and *Better Call Saul*. Shishir said that while he knew the giant magnetic truck wouldn't be in evidence at Twisters, visiting the restaurant in person was nonnegotiable: "It's iconic. It's where Gus had his mini HQ!"

Spice up your life with an order of Chile Cheese Fries, Christmas sauce.

QUARTERS

$

Quarters BBQ is permanently closed. Quarters Discount Liquors, on the same lot, remains open.
801 Yale Blvd. SE, Albuquerque, 87106
(505) 247-8579
Sunday, 11:00 a.m.–4:00 p.m.
Monday–Saturday, 9:00 a.m.–9:00 p.m.

BB s2.e12, "Phoenix," May 24, 2009

Walt orders a Fat Tire draft at Quarters after delivering Jesse his money. Jesse and Jane are high, and Walt is confident all that cash is just headed for more drugs. He speaks with Skyler on the phone, telling her he can't find diapers in the right size but he's off to Walmart to check for more. This is obviously not the case because he's sitting down for a beer. Who should say "well played" but Donald Margolis (John de Lancie), the father of Jesse's girlfriend, Jane Margolis (Krysten Ritter). Don is already halfway through his draft and has an empty shot glass too. We aren't sure what he's drinking.

FIGURE 15. Quarters Discount Liquors exterior, 2022. Courtesy of Aimee Macpherson.

The conversation starts with the news from the little TV behind the bar—water on Mars—and drifts to how worried they are about young family members. Unbeknown to the other, Walt is talking about Jesse and Don is talking about Jane. After that fateful conversation, possibly inspired by Don's remark that you never give up on them, Walt returns to the flat where Jesse and Jane are sleeping and, well . . . you know what happens next.

Fat Tire Amber Ale is a beer that gets its name from fat bike tires, the kind used on mountain bikes for longer bikepacking trips.[9] The beer has undergone a makeover since it was featured in *Breaking Bad*. The Fat Tire beer that Walt drank tasted syrupy with a malt tang, but it is no longer an amber; as of early 2023, the recipe changed to a lighter beer, closer to a lager in taste. The packaging has also changed. The old Fat tire was a brown glass bottle with a red bicycle at the center of a navy-and-red label and serif font. Today the bicycle is blue with a red sun behind it, and the font is sans serif. The container is now a can with a mostly white color.

Quarters in real life had a wide-angled bar top and wood paneling true to the 1970s vibe of Quarters on-screen. Today, only the liquor store remains open to the public. In February 2022, after fifty years, the bar and barbecue restaurant closed. The packaged liquor store is located two doors up from the closed restaurant. It is a big store with an extensive selection of alcohol.

Swing by Quarters Discount Liquors and pick up a six-pack of Fat Tire.

ISLETA RESORT & CASINO $$

a.k.a. Serenity
11000 Broadway Blvd. SE, Albuquerque, 87105
(505) 724-3800
isleta.com
Sunday–Saturday, 6:00 a.m.–8:00 p.m.

BB s2.e13, "ABQ," May 31, 2009
BB s3.e1, "No Más," March 21, 2010
BB s5.e12, "Rabid Dog," September 1, 2013

Isleta Resort & Casino wears several hats in the world of *Breaking Bad*. In season 2's "ABQ," Walt takes Jesse here to recover after his drug binge that followed the death of his girlfriend, Jane. It's a milestone episode because we are introduced to the character of Mike Ehrmantraut. He's hired by Walt to remove drug evidence from Jesse's apartment and to coach Jesse on how to interact with the police. We next see Jesse in what looks like a world away, sitting in a bathrobe by the outdoor pool. But it's clear his mind is still fully immersed in the memory of his recent trauma. Walt's ominous presence by the pool only adds to the tension between what on the

FIGURE 16. Isleta Resort & Casino's Jar Spa interior, as Serenity rehabilitation center, *BB* s2.e13 "ABQ" (2009). Courtesy of Sony Pictures Television.

surface should look relaxing (beautiful views, nice pool, robe) but is for Jesse a deeply unpleasant experience. In “No Más” in season 3, Jesse is back at this location, now fleshed out as Serenity, a drug rehab facility.

In season 5, the Isleta is also used as the exterior of the hotel where Walt relocates with his family after Jesse tries to burn down their house. “Rabid Dog” shows Walt in a contemplative mood by the pool, mirroring Jesse’s contemplation of his low point in “ABQ.” While Walt is at the hotel, both Skyler and Saul suggest that Walt have Jesse bumped off, but Walt refuses. Walt poignantly decides to keep Jesse alive at the same location that he brought Jesse to in order to keep him alive several seasons ago. Walt is certainly capable of hurting Jesse, and Jesse does his best to try hurt Walt, but in the end it seems like they are currently doing a better job of keeping each other alive.

The interior hotel rooms at Isleta weren’t used the show; the White family hotel rooms were sets built at the studio. It’s common practice for TV production to break up locations in this way. It provides more flexibility in the shooting schedule and allows for more creativity in the camerawork of a small room. You can build wild walls on a stage that can be moved out of the way for the camera, which is impossible on location. You can also have the set at your disposal for days when you have to reschedule at the last moment due to inclement weather or actor availability. We see this technique used in several reoccurring locations in *Breaking Bad* and *Better Call Saul*.

In real life, Isleta Resort & Casino is a huge property. Located on the Pueblo of Isleta in the Rio Grande Valley, the resort is owned by the people after whom it is named. A casino has been in operation on the site since 1986,[10] although the property has undergone substantial renovations since then. The hotel overlooks the Rio Grande bosque at the foot of the Sandia Mountains. The resort boasts an indoor and an outdoor pool (Walt and Jesse are both spotted at the outdoor pool in “ABQ.”) The resort’s spa is in the unique onion-shaped building that serves as a place marker for Jesse’s rehab center on the show. This unique building is called the Jar Spa and features a rain shower that flows into a hot tub at the center of the room.[11] There is a poolside drink service, but no alcohol is permitted when gambling on the casino floor. There is a golf course, bowling alley, and multiple eating venues in addition to the casino and hotel. Embers Steak & Seafood, Chile Ristra food court, and Chill Ice Cream & Coffee Bar offer a range of options for every budget. Smoking is no longer permitted on the casino floor.

Order an iced coffee from Chill for a pick-me-up at the slots.

NOTES

1. johnny_mango, "One More Click on the Big Clock: The Burt's Tiki Lounge Neon about to Bite the Dust," *Albloggerque* (blog), March 31, 2019, http://albloggerque.blogspot.com/2019/03/one-more-click-on-big-clock-burts-tiki.html.

2. Wikipedia, s.v. "Western False Fronts," last modified October 3, 2023, 06:12, https://en.wikipedia.org/wiki/Western_false_front_architecture.

3. *Merriam-Webster*, s.v. "false front (*n.*)," accessed March 31, 2022, https://www.merriam-webster.com/dictionary/false%20front.

4. Savoy Bar & Grill, "About Us," accessed March 28, 2022, http://savoyabq.com/about-us/.

5. Ann Abel, "Why Albuquerque, New Mexico, Is the Most Exotic American Big City," *Forbes*, May 11, 2021, https://www.forbes.com/sites/annabel/2021/05/11/why-albuquerque-new-x-mexico-is-the-most-exotic-american-big-city/?sh=5f153cf2a935.

6. Dirty Bourbon, "All About Us," accessed March 28, 2022, https://thedirtybourbon.com/about-us.

7. Guy Debord, *The Society of the Spectacle*, English ed. by Ron. Adams (Cambridge: Unredacted Word, 2021); also available at https://unredacted-word.pub/spectacle/.

8. Visit Albuquerque, "Barelas/South Valley," accessed March 31, 2022, https://www.visitalbuquerque.org/about-abq/neighborhoods/south-valley/.

9. Fat Tire, "Classic Ale: Fat Tire," accessed January 26, 2024, https://www.newbelgium.com/beer/fat-tire/.

10. Christine Faria, “Isleta Resort & Casino,” *Tribal Gaming and Hospitality*, Winter 2020, https://tgandh.com/articles/special-X-features/isleta-resort-casino/.

11. Isleta Resort & Casino, “The Spa,” accessed March 28, 2022, https://www.isleta.com/spa/.

BLAKE'S LOTABURGER

$

Blake's Lotaburger takeout food and packaging
3207 Richmond Dr. NE, Albuquerque, 87107
(505) 884-2530
lotaburger.com
Monday–Friday, 6:00 a.m.–3:00 p.m.

BB s3.e2, "Caballo sin Nombre," March 28, 2010
BB s3.e12, "Half Measures," June 6, 2010

Building—a.k.a. Los Pollos Hermanos Restaurant #2 (permanently closed)
6301 Gibson Blvd. SE, Albuquerque, 87108

BCS s5.e7, "JMM," March 30, 2020
BCS s5.e10, "Something Unforgivable," April 20, 2020

In *Breaking Bad*, Blake's food packaging with its iconic red, white, and blue to-go bag is used by a variety of characters. In *Better Call Saul*, a closed Blake's restaurant is used as a location for a Twisters that is blown to bits.

FIGURE 17. Skyler drinks a Blake's Lotaburger soda, *BB* s3.e2, "Caballo sin Nombre" (2010). Courtesy of Sony Pictures Television.

FIGURE 18. Blake's soda, 2023. Courtesy of Aimee Macpherson.

FIGURE 19. Exterior of Blake's on Richmond, 2023. Courtesy of Aimee Macpherson.

Skyler White was a fan of Blake's. In *Breaking Bad*'s "Caballo sin Nombre," she slurps from one of their large-sized beverage containers. Skyler shares a Blake's takeout meal with Hank Schrader (Dean Norris) and Walter "Flynn" White Jr. (R. J. Mitte). Her sister, Marie, is also at the table, but she has a plate of sushi because, as she says, "I've had enough trans fat for one lifetime." In "Half Measures," sex worker and meth addict Wendy S. (Julia Minesci) holds a rumpled Blake's bag at the end of the opening montage. She saunters over to a parked car, holding the bag to the tune of "Windy" by the Association. Handing the Blake's bag and some cash to the dealers, she gets meth in return. Next time we see her holding a Blake's bag, Wendy is sitting in Jesse Pinkman's red 1982 Chevrolet Monte Carlo. The bag holds two burgers that Jesse poisoned with ricin. Mike and Victor (Jeremiah Bitsui) find Jesse and Wendy before the drug dealers arrive at their usual spot. Mike gets Jesse out of his car, instructing Wendy to take a walk. She gets out, still holding the Blake's bag. The poisoned burgers are never delivered, nor are the burgers themselves featured on-screen.

For the uninitiated, Blake's is a New Mexican fast-food joint that sells burgers and fries, breakfast items, shakes, and more. The restaurant's standout graphics make its locations easy to spot throughout the city. In *Better Call Saul* season 5, you can see the curved windows of an old Blake's building, complete with a red trim on the cornices above. The iconic Blake's packaging featured on *Breaking Bad* has since changed: now the logo can only be found on the large-sized cups, and their to-go bags are now made from undyed brown paper. This means your homage to Wendy or Skyler will look slightly different from the on-screen product. But that's no reason to forgo the tasty local franchise.

Blake's makes their substantial breakfast burritos with real scrambled eggs (not a mix from a carton). With generous portions of sausage, bacon, or carne adovada, this handheld breakfast will keep you full a ways down I-40. Something a little different for breakfast that still has a New Mexican twist is the LOTA Breakfast Sandwich, served on Texas-style toast, which is twice as thick as an average slice of white bread, with a crisped exterior and a light and fluffy inside. The sandwich is filled with two eggs any style and a choice of sausage or bacon, cheese (American), and red or green chile. If you're eating in the car, I'd say the scrambled-egg-and-sausage sandwich holds its physical integrity for longer. But if you're eating right away, bacon provides just the right amount of salted crunch to contrast with the slow burn of soft, smoky green chile. Marry that with over-easy eggs and you will need some paper napkins to mop up the extremely satisfying aftermath.

Look out for the many signs outside Blake's restaurants in Albuquerque. Easily spotted from the road, the older signs feature a guy with a tall hat and striped coat, smiling as he holds a banner that says "Blake's," written in red italicized brush script. The man's legs are poles that form the A-frame base of the sign. Eyeballing the structure, it's around fifteen feet tall, and clearly visible from a distance on one of Albuquerque's wide boulevards. I like to go to the Blake's at 3207 Richmond Drive NE because it's got many old-school features, like the Blake's man outside, decorative ironwork on the exterior, and small diner stools inside. It's also right next to the Blake's training center. Outside, there are often large parked trucks with Blake's decals on the side that include the cheeky slogan "Where are they taking me?"

The business was started as a burger stand by American businessman Blake Chanslor in 1952, right here in Albuquerque. The restaurant chain is credited with popularizing the use of green chile on burgers.[1] The LOTA Burger "New Mexico Style" comes with two all-beef patties, melty American cheese, and Hatch green chile. Chile is now so popular on burgers in New Mexico that it's unusual to find a beef patty without it. The LOTA Burger comes with a single patty, no chile. "LOTA's little brother," ITSA Burger, is a very manageable, smaller version of its LOTA counterpart. Blake's Frito Pie is comforting and fresh, and the Loaded Chili Cheese Fries come with Texas-style chili—ground beef sautéed in tomato with spices—and straight, not curly, fries. (This dish is entirely different from the Chile Cheese Fries found at Twisters, which come with curly fries and your choice of red or green chile, or both.)

Blake's has a variety of beverages to keep you satiated, ranging from milk and chocolate milk to lemonade, sweet tea, and fountain drinks—i.e., drinks that come from a soda fountain, including Pepsi, Dr Pepper, and their diet versions, plus Mountain Dew. Translation: no Coca-Cola.

We're all familiar with the *Breaking Bad* chicken restaurant, which you can visit at Isleta, but let's not overlook the second location featured in season 5 of *Better Call Saul*. In "JMM," Lalo Salamanca (Tony Dalton) makes an illegal call to Ignacio "Nacho" Varga (Michael Mando) from jail. His instructions are to burn down a Los Pollos Hermanos restaurant. Nacho informs Gus of Lalo's instructions. Gus is keen to maintain Nacho's cover as a mole in Lalo's organization—to that end, Gus not only goes to one of his restaurants with Nacho but performs the arson himself, torching his own restaurant with characteristic precision and panache. Using a frozen chicken, boiling fryer oil, and a makeshift conveyor belt, Gus creates an impressive explosion. The house props are simple everyday materials, but with a few in-camera tricks from the *Better Call Saul* props and special effects departments, they transformed into something much more dangerous than fast food.

As if to prove the show's commitment to in-camera effects, we revisit the burned-out restaurant later in the season during episode 10, "Something Unforgivable," where it provides the background to Mike and Gus's daytime meeting. The damage to the restaurant is visible as Mike informs Gus that both Nacho and Lalo are headed south to Chihuahua, Mexico. Mike advocates for releasing Nacho from his duties as a double agent, but Gus rejects the suggestion. As for the restaurant in the background, it's clear the place took a beating from the hot oil and frozen chicken explosion.

Story-wise in *Better Call Saul*, this restaurant is located in the village of Los Lunas, Valencia County, just south of Albuquerque. In real life, the building is an old Blake's Lotaburger in Albuquerque proper. If you've watched the "JMM" episode, it will come as no surprise that this location is closed for business. This defunct restaurant has a "for lease" sign outside, but for now, it's just sitting there on Gibson, waiting for you to drive by, take a selfie, and think of how Gus's evil genius is so creative that even a single dead chicken becomes an instrument of mayhem in his hands. Fun fact regarding this episode: it was written and directed by women. Alison Tatlock wrote the script and longtime executive producer Melissa Bernstein directed it. This was Melissa's directing debut on the show, and I think we can all agree it started with a bang!

There are many Lotaburger restaurants to choose from across the city of Albuquerque. Order a LOTA Burger "New Mexico Style." Wash it down with a fountain drink to get the cup like Skyler's. Order to go for a bag like Wendy's.

GINO'S NEW YORK STYLE PIZZA $$

Formerly Venezia's Pizzeria
3908 San Mateo Blvd. NE, Albuquerque, 87110
(505) 883-6000
ginosnystylepizza.com
Sunday–Thursday, 11:00 a.m.–9:00 p.m.
Friday–Saturday, 11:00 a.m.–10:00 p.m.

BB s3.e2, "Caballo sin Nombre" March 28, 2010
BB s4.e2, "Thirty-Eight Snub," July 24, 2011
BCS s4.e2, "Breathe," August 13, 2018
BCS s4.e3, "Something Beautiful," August 20, 2018

"Caballo sin Nombre"—what an episode. You know I'm not going to be talking about a horse. TV's most famous pizza was made at Venezia's Pizzeria in Albuquerque, renamed Gino's New York Style Pizza after the original owner retired and his nephews took over the business.[2] Gino's website has a little story from the current owner about their experiences with the show and just how many pies they baked for the scenes. Just DBAA and try to throw a pie on Walter White's roof.

FIGURE 20. Walt throws a pie from Venezia's Pizzeria (now called Gino's New York Style Pizza), *BB* s3.e2, "Caballo sin Nombre" (2010). Courtesy of Sony Pictures Television.

FIGURE 21. Gino's pizza exterior, 2022. Courtesy of Aimee Macpherson.

FIGURE 22. Gino's pizza in a box, 2022. Courtesy of Aimee Macpherson.

The restaurant itself is simple, the cutlery is disposable, and the dining tables are well worn. It's hard not to fall in love with the plastic-protected photos of the old country on the dining tables in the indoor seating area. They also make a speedy trade at the drive-through, if you prefer pizza on the run.

I ordered a small cheese pizza, and it was served piping hot in the signature cardboard box. From my seat, I could see the staff slide the pie straight from the industrial pizza oven onto red-and-white checkered paper lining the open box, swiftly close it, and then deliver it my greedy, outstretched hands. It's easily recognizable as a New York–style pizza: The dough is tossed by hand. The center of the pie is thin, while the crust is thick and chewy thanks to the addition of salt to the dough. A thin, evenly distributed layer of grated mozzarella covers a gently acidic marinara base. The pie is thin enough for you to stack two slices on top of each other.

In "Caballo sin Nombre," Walt brings dinner home to his family and proudly notes that he's got "dipping sticks" as well as a pizza. (Gino's menu does not offer "dipping sticks" by name but does have a side order of breadsticks that comes with house-made sauce.) The YouTube clip of Walt subsequently hurling the pizza onto the roof of his family's home, posted by the official Breaking Bad & Better Call Saul channel, has 1.5 million views and over three thousand comments. It has twenty-five thousand "likes" and zero dislikes.[3] The stats speak for themselves. This TV moment, emblematic of the unique tone and voice of *Breaking Bad*, is nestled deep in the hearts of many fans. It's goofy, sinister, relatable, and completely surreal all at once. By the time Walt is removing the pie from the roof, I think it's clear that he's learning how unpleasant it can be to clean up your own mess—but the show stops short of making Walt eat "humble pie."

Obviously, the roof of a house is a strange place for pizza to end up. But Walt's new skill set, too, is uncanny. His new life has shifted his experiences outside the realm of familiar and normal. So it's almost hilarious to watch this criminal mastermind trying to be normal. Walt performing the "Aw, shucks, what's the big deal, let's just sit down and eat together" shtick just doesn't come across as sincere. He's so aggressive with the ridiculously large pizza box, trying to force his way through the doorframe, that the situation becomes tainted with menace. It's clear he's convinced himself he can intimidate Skyler into taking a deal the way Heisenberg can intimidate drug dealers.

The pizza itself is a pepperoni and is perhaps most famous for being unsliced; a sliced pizza would fall apart midair and ruin the gag. In real life, of course, ordering unsliced pizza pie to go is unusual. To address the reason why unsliced pizza is the norm in the *Breaking Bad* universe, season 4's "Thirty-Eight Snub" features a scene where Badger (Matt Jones) carries into a party a stack of large pizza boxes bearing the Venezia logo. When the top pizza box is opened, Jesse immediately comments, "Yo, what's up with the pie, man? It ain't cut." Badger explains that it's Venezia's way of "passing the savings on to you." Vince Gilligan did a Reddit AMA session and answered a question on this from "pee_diddy" that confirms the writers included the season 4 explanation to avoid the "audience's righteous wrath!"[4]

According to the story calendar, *Better Call Saul*'s "Breathe" is the first time Gino's makes an appearance in the show's universe. But of course, Mr. Neff (Andrew Friedman) ordering pizza with the line "Could you throw in some dipping sticks?" is a big Easter egg for all those *Breaking Bad* fans enamored with the famous unsliced pizza. Ira (Franc Ross), the professional burglar and owner of Vamonos Pest, is hiding under Mr. Neff's desk as he dials in the order. This episode is the first time since *Breaking Bad* that viewers catch sight of Ira.

Get a large, unsliced pepperoni pizza for the authentic prop. But if you're planning to eat it, I'd 100 percent recommend getting it sliced or bringing a pair of scissors. Eat it indoors, outdoors, or on the go via the drive-through.

LEO'S NIGHTCLUB $

1119 Candelaria Rd. NW, Albuquerque, 87107
(505) 341-9564
facebook.com/people/Leos-Nightclub/100063774451461
Sunday, 12:00 p.m.–11:45 p.m.
Monday–Thursday, 12:00 p.m.–12:00 a.m.
Friday–Saturday, 12:00 p.m.–1:45 a.m.

BB s3.e3, "I.F.T.," April 4, 2010

Hank and his Drug Enforcement Administration (DEA) partner, Steven Gomez (Steven Michael Quezada), visit Leo's on a sunny afternoon. The scene opens with their order: a huge, soggy plate of nachos served in a basket lined with tinfoil. Gomez isn't complimentary about the location, wondering aloud, "What are we doing in this shithole?" and wishes they'd gone to Chili's, the Tex-Mex family restaurant chain, or Mac's, a locally owned steak house that has "that green onion." (Mac's Steak in the Rough is a New Mexico fast-food joint that serves deep-fried steak fingers with fries, white gravy, and a green onion. They have one location remaining in Albuquerque, at 4515 Menaul Boulevard NE, 87110.) But this bar is exactly where Hank wants to be. The

FIGURE 23. Leo's Nightclub exterior, *BB* s3.e3, "I.F.T" (2010). Courtesy of Sony Pictures Television.

FIGURE 24. Leo's zero-tolerance policy, 2023. Courtesy of Aimee Macpherson.

FIGURE 25. Leo's michelada, 2023. Courtesy of Aimee Macpherson.

pressures at work and home have sent him looking for trouble. Hank finds it by provoking a brawl at the bar with some bikers who appear to make a drug deal at one of the tables.

In real life, Leo's is occasionally frequented by vintage car enthusiasts and has plenty of live and lively events, such as karaoke every Wednesday, and a regular rotation of conjunto norteño bands.[5] The other week, they had a DJ session dedicated to mariachi singer Chente (a.k.a. Vicente Fernández). Check out their Facebook page for events; there is typically a cover charge if a live band is playing. The bar is well stocked with plenty of classics. I think the venue is best described in its own words: "GREAT TIME AND A PARTY PLACE TO BE CHICHICHOU!!!!"[6]

I also visited Leo's on a sunny afternoon. Over ten years since its feature on *Breaking Bad*, the building's exterior has changed. The emergency exit door we see Hank leave through is now at the side of the building rather than the back under an awning. In place of the exit sign and push door you see in shot behind Gomez there is now a wall with a poster on it of a woman's naked behind. On the bottom is a stein of beer with the words "This one's on me." Outside, the dumpster we see on-screen was moved to make way for more parking space. The dumpster is now by the muraled wall opposite the bar in the parking lot. Officially, you enter through the front door that faces Candelaria Road. Nailed to the open corrugated iron gates at the entrance there is a sign detailing the bar's zero-tolerance policy regarding drugs, weapons, and the like. To the right of the entrance is a closed food truck called Tacos y Montados El Viejon. *Montados* are a Chihuahuan style of burrito. *Viejón* is slang for "elderly." Behind the truck are signs advertising nightclub fun: "Drink Screwball here!" and "Let's party!"

Inside, the venue is split into three different zones. On the left as you walk in are many pool tables. To the right is a wide bar and seating area (where Hank and Gomez sit) and to the far right is a wood dance floor with half a dozen loudspeakers and several spotlights. Immediately to your left as you enter is a vending machine with single-use vapes in a variety of flavors for twenty dollars a pop. I got to Leo's about half an hour after the bar opened and it was filling up with a dozen or so customers. Two of the pool tables were in use. Leaning against the bar top were two gentlemen in square-toed boots and palm straw hats drinking Modelo Especial from glass bottles. A lady was taking her cocktail to a high table as I passed. She wore a long, black collared shirt; underneath was a cropped halter top, also in black, with the phrase "Fuck You" printed on the front in yellow-and-red flamed font. I sat toward the end of the bar and ordered a *michelada* made with Modelo Especial. The bartender quickly set up the tomato juice and beer cocktail, fixing Tajín around the rim of a large, wide-lipped goblet with a faded Coors logo printed on the side and lodging two tiny black straws into the ice so they didn't bounce out of the drink. Once the tomato juice was in, she opened the beer in front of me, poured some into the goblet and left the remaining beer in bottle. Both were placed on the bar top, whose varnish was peeling. The drink was lit by pendulum lights hanging along the length of the bar, their shades made from used Patrón tequila bottles. It tasted like a classic michelada, refreshing and tangy without being too heavy on the booze. While enjoying my beverage, I watched part of an NBA game projected onto the back wall of the bar area.

Head to Leo's for a refreshing drink, live music, or a game of pool.

SANDIA BAR

$

a.k.a. bar in Mexico (temporarily closed)
4445 Corrales Rd., Corrales, 87048

BB s3.e3, "I.F.T.," April 4, 2010

The "I.F.T." episode opens at another bar, which is currently closed. Story-wise the bar is located in Mexico. In real life, Sandia Bar is located in the village of Corrales, right outside Albuquerque. On the show, Tortuga (Danny Trejo) has a cigar, drinks some booze, and is delighted with a surprise visit from cartel underboss Don Juan Bolsa (Javier Grajeda). A running theme for this episode is the uncomplimentary bar reviews. Juan calls Tortuga's drinking hole a "culo de burro" and lures him to a back room to look at his birthday present (yes, your alarm bells should be ringing). It's an enormous tortoise, which Tortuga is pleased to see until Bolsa paints "Hola DEA" on its shell. Shortly after receiving his present, Tortuga's head is hacked off in the back room by one of the cartel cousins as punishment for working with DEA agent Hank Schrader.

Sandia Bar is, or was, a real bar at the time the episode aired in 2010. At the time of writing, it is closed but local news hints that it may reopen. In the summer of 2022, the Corrales Planning and Zoning Commission approved plans to double the bar's square footage and add outside seating and a performance stage.[7] I don't have a forecast for the opening date, but check the news in the *Rio Rancho Observer* for any updates. It's too soon to know how much of the original bar, where Tortuga sat, is going to change during the renovation.

4'S CABARET $

4's Cabaret (permanently closed)
2294 Wyoming Blvd. NE, Albuquerque, 87112
Billiard Palace (open business attached to the closed location)

2288 Wyoming Blvd. NE, Albuquerque, 87112
(505) 323-6800
Sunday, 12:00 p.m.–12:00 a.m.
Monday–Saturday, 11:00 a.m.–1:00 a.m.

BB s3.e5, "Más," April 18, 2010

4's Cabaret was a real strip club back when "Más" aired in 2010. Today this address, located in a strip mall up in the Northeast Heights with a very generous parking lot, appears, to all intents and purposes, closed. Instead of the dark-gray walls and red doors featured on the show, the exterior is painted taupe. The roof is covered in warped wood tiles. To the left of the building is a JOANN fabric and craft store. To the right, inset behind an extremely

FIGURE 26. 4's Cabaret exterior, 2023. Courtesy of Aimee Macpherson.

FIGURE 27. Billiard Palace exterior, 2023. Courtesy of Aimee Macpherson.

green strip of lawn, is a pool hall called Billiard Palace. The business's exterior windows are covered in images of scantily clad women on the beach advertising beers such as Tecate and Miller Lite. Inside are more pool tables than I can count; the floor is carpeted and there is no natural light. When I visited around noon, the pool tables were starting to fill up with a crowd of silver-haired gentlemen. At the bar, a couple were discussing an ex-girlfriend. The pool hall shares a wall with the former strip club and a popular Village Inn restaurant.

On-screen, 4's Cabaret provides a brief but memorable flashback scene with Jesse, Skinny Pete, and Combo: Walt gives Jesse his life savings to buy an RV. Jesse takes that money and spends most of it at the strip club with his friends. When Jesse realizes what he's done, Combo sources him a cheap RV in a "no-paperwork type deal" (read, stealing it from his mom's driveway). Hank's search for that very same RV lands him at Combo's mother's house, where he sees a photo of Combo and Jesse from the strip club that infamous night. It's this photo that gives Hank the scent for Jesse. 4's Cabaret was on air in 2010. The next time we see a strip club in the

Breaking Bad / *Better Call Saul* universe is in *Better Call Saul* season 4, episode 8, "Coushatta," which aired in 2018.

4's is no longer in business and the building isn't open to the general public. Once you've clocked the exterior, head next door to the Billiard Palace to shoot some pool.

NOTES

1. Wikipedia, s.v. "Blake's Lotaburger," last modified October 15, 2023, 08:41, https://en.wikipedia.org/wiki/Blake%27s_Lotaburger.
2. Gino's New York Style Pizza, "Breaking Bad," accessed March 18, 2022, https://www.ginosnystylepizza.com/breaking-bad.html.
3. Breaking Bad & Better Call Saul, "Pizza on the Roof, Caballo sin Nombre, Breaking Bad," August 10, 2018, YouTube video, 2:39, https://www.youtube.com/watch?v=Bg6dxhJbq78&ab_channel=BreakingBad%26BetterCallSaul.
4. Reddit, AMA, "I Am Vince Gilligan, Creator of Breaking Bad and Co-creator of Better Call Saul," accessed March 17, 2017, https://www.reddit.com/r/television/comments/5zrxsx/i_am_vince_gilligan_creator_of_breaking_bad_and/.
5. Berklee Pulse, "Introduction to Mexican Music: Conjunto Norteño Music," accessed August 1, 2022, https://pulse.berklee.edu/?id=4&lesson=30&book=410&chapter=3838.
6. Leo's Nightclub Facebook page, accessed September 8, 2022, https://www.facebook.com/people/Leos-Nightclub/100063774451461/.
7. Maureen Cooke, "Sandia Bar Approved by Planning Board," *Rio Rancho Observer*, July 27, 2022, https://rrobserver.com/sandia-bar-approved-by-planning-board-was-featured-in-breaking-bad/.

DENNY'S

$

Shooting location (permanently closed)
2608 Central Ave. SE, Albuquerque, 87106
New location

1620 Towne Center Ln. SE, Albuquerque, 87106
(505) 242-6057
locations.dennys.com/NM/ALBUQUERQUE/248881
Sunday–Saturday, open 24 hours

BB s4.e1, "Box Cutter," July 17, 2011
BB s5.e1, "Live Free or Die," July 15, 2012
BB s5.e16, "Felina," September 29, 2013

The Denny's restaurant featured in *Breaking Bad* closed in 2014. The *Albuquerque Journal* gives it all away with the headline "Losing an Institution."[1] Jackie Sandoval, one of the owners of the Breaking Bad RV Tours with her husband, Frank, is quoted in the article, "I know a lot of fans are truly heartbroken over (the closure). . . . It's crazy." The site is now a strip mall with a Chipotle and a Jersey Mike's. So forget going to the exact spot like you can at the Dog House.

FIGURE 28. Walt's breakfast at Denny's, BB s5.e1, "Live Free or Die" (2012). Courtesy of Sony Pictures Television.

FIGURE 29. Denny's breakfast, 2022. Courtesy of Aimee Macpherson.

The Valero gas station captured on-screen outside Denny's has also moved, making it hard to re-create the exterior shot. The Chipotle parking lot seems to be mostly untouched from the Denny's days, when Walt parked there in "Live Free or Die." At this point, Walt has sold the 2004 Pontiac Aztec for the famously ridiculous price of fifty dollars, and he's abandoned in the desert the brand-new leased black Chrysler 300C SRT-8 (*Breaking Bad* s5.e6, "Buyout"). (In season 5's "Felina," he drives to Denny's in a stolen 1986 white Volvo 240 with New Hampshire plates. We all know why. He drives away in a red—looks like more of a burnt umber to me—1977 Cadillac DeVille with New Mexico plates.) You can park your car like Walt, nose facing Central, and catch the view of the University of New Mexico campus that Jesse and Walt see from their diner booth in "Box Cutter." New Mexico's exceptionally dry climate is great for preserving old cars, so look out for vintage Volvos and Cadillacs. You might just get lucky and see one like Walt's.

Where does this leave die-hard fans looking to re-create Walter White's famously sad birthday meal from "Live Free or Die"? Regarding the infamous breakfast, you have two choices. Choice one: do it yourself. There's a stressful YouTube video channel called the Last Supper[2] created by an English guy, who re-creates this meal from scratch in his kitchen, wearing what he describes as a "giant yellow condom" as an homage to the yellow hazmat suits donned by Walt and Jesse. It involves grating potatoes. You don't have to do this. Please read on.

Choice two is much simpler. Just head out to one of three Denny's locations in Albuquerque—for example, Denny's at 1620 Towne Center Lane SE. Franchisees Yashna and Sham Asnani operated the Denny's featured in *Breaking Bad*, and when corporate decided close that location, it had them move to the new Denny's on Towne Center Lane.[3] The diner's interior is modern and light. I took a seat by the window and pulled down the blind to protect my eyes from the blast of the New Mexico summer heat. I chose to replicate Walt's breakfast. To do that from the real Denny's menu of today, I ordered from the "Build Your Own Grand Slam" section of the menu. Hash browns, two orders of bacon, and two eggs. (Walt orders his eggs sunny-side up, but I chose mine over easy because that's my personal preference, and who wants to waste eggs?) I showed the server a screenshot of Walt's plate, but she hadn't had many diners come in to replicate the experience. Although the restaurant wasn't too crowded, many people were ordering from the to-go counter. My coffee, fresh and hot, was served in a white curved mug with the C-style handle. The insulation on the mug was decent even though it wasn't the old-school, thick diner mug we see Walt drink from. It had the Denny's logo on one side and "It's Fry O'Clock Somewhere" printed in red on the other side. My breakfast came quickly—the eggs were cooked in butter, and the bacon was soft. Snapping the pieces to create the number 52 wasn't possible, but I could tear them easily. My place mat was a colored paper rectangle advertising jobs.

Leaving the meal untouched along with a hundred-dollar bill as a tip is probably totally off budget for most people, including me. But if you can afford to, why not? What a cool way to pay homage to the show and make someone's day in the process. Lucy was the name of the Denny's waitress in *Breaking Bad*, and she was played by Albuquerque-born actress Monique Candelaria.

"Boxcutter" in season 4 shows Jesse at Denny's ordering pancakes with bacon plus sausage; it looks like he is served whipped butter and syrup, but he only uses some of the syrup. After slurping down what looks like an ice tea, he asks the server for a refill. Across from him, Walt just has an old diner-style mug of black coffee in front of him. The discrepancy between the two is just another way of showing rather than telling us how differently the two characters process their violent and brutal actions.

Denny's itself has gone through something of an interior design remodel. Gone are the jazzy purple upholstered benches and brown-rimmed plates featured on *Breaking Bad*. Instead, you will see red vinyl benches and plain white plates. You'll be pleased to know that their pancakes, black coffee, bacon, eggs, and even hash browns remain very similar to how they looked in the early 2000s, so the meal you order is going to look like the one you see on TV. By season 5's "Live Free or Die," Walt's behavior has obviously left him a changed man and it's hardly a surprise that he's unable to find comfort in re-creating a benign, low-key family tradition—marking birthday numbers with bacon. But you on the other hand can forget Walt's terrible acts of inhumanity and just focus on the simple pleasure of an inexpensive and freshly cooked breakfast.

Before *Breaking Bad*, Denny's was a muse for Wim Wenders, as shown with his photo *Always Open, Needles California* featured in his book *Written in the West*.[4] This book is a compilation of photos Wenders took in preparation for his film *Paris, Texas* (1984). His snap of Denny's gave the diner an association with postmodern Americana long before Walt and Jesse stride through the door. Wenders's book covers New Mexico, California, Arizona, and Texas. In an interview with Alain Bergala, published in the book, he describes New Mexico as "God forsaken." Appropriately enough, he then goes on to explain why that is appealing to his camera: "I often chose locations because I knew they were disappearing. . . . Behind the photos is a wish to look at something (*regarder*) and to preserve it (*garder*). The French word gets it nicely: *re-garder*. The photos Walter Evans took during the Depression were just that: preserving something that was going to disappear in three or four years' time, in your eye and in your memory."[5]

Consider Denny's in this context and the restaurant has a more complex cinematic legacy than the Grand Slamwich breakfast special would have you believe.[6]

For a taste of Walt's breakfast, order from the "Build Your Own Grand Slam" section, with two extra sides of bacon, two eggs sunny-side up, hash browns, and black coffee.

LOUIE'S PUB AND GRILL $

5603 Menaul Blvd. NE, Albuquerque, 87110
(505) 881-5333
louiespubgrill.com
Sunday, 11:00 a.m.–8:00 p.m.
Monday–Saturday, 11:00 a.m.–12:00 a.m.

BB s4.e2, "Thirty-Eight Snub," July 24, 2011
BCS s2.e9, "Nailed," April 11, 2016
BCS s4.e8, "Coushatta," September 24, 2018
BCS s5.e3, "The Guy for This," March 2, 2020

This location is an example of an Easter egg showing up more frequently on *Better Call Saul* then it was ever featured on *Breaking Bad*, where the location was first established. In *Breaking Bad*'s "Thirty-Eight Snub," we see Mike at Louie's twice. First, he drinks coffee at the bar. He wipes Victor's blood from his jacket. The mood is calm. Second, Walt comes to Mike and suggests they are in "the same boat" against Gus—i.e., "Can you schedule a meeting so I can kill him?" As a response, Mike knocks Walt down and gives him a brutal few kicks in the gut. Louie's is Mike Ehrmantraut's place.

FIGURE 30. Louie's Pub & Grill sign, 2022. Courtesy of Aimee Macpherson.

FIGURE 31. Santa Fe Brewing Company 7K IPA at Louie's, 2022. Courtesy of Aimee Macpherson.

In *Better Call Saul*, we get a deeper look into Mike and his family, so it makes sense that the show allows us to see the full spectrum of his character at this pub—deadpan, sensitive, easygoing, and violent as hell. In season 4's "Coushatta," Werner Ziegler, the German engineer, and Mike sit at the bar. Wermer schools a fellow patron on the correct pronunciation of "hefeweizen," a Bavarian-style wheat beer. This is probably as close as we'll ever get to seeing Mike performing a male bonding ritual. We see his conviviality with Werner is sincere. Obviously, a lot has happened between "Coushatta," and when we next see Mike at the bar in season 5's "The Guy for This." Clearly, Werner's death really stings Mike. He's upset and emotional—a rarity for this character. All that's happened to Mike during *Better Call Saul* gives us new insight into his behavior in *Breaking Bad*'s "Thirty-Eight Snub." We knew he was a tough guy, but now we also know more about some of the painful memories he has buried inside. Mike contains so much more than his hard-boiled exterior will have you believe.

Louie's is a local pub with a loving following (check out Howie K.'s detailed review on Yelp[7]). It's throwing distance from a Fed Ex shipping center, a hearing aid store, and a smoke shop. Incidentally it's also very close to the location where the CC Mobile store was filmed (*BCS* s4.e4, "Talk," 5805 Menaul Blvd. NE, Albuquerque, 87110). There are plenty of modern breweries here in Albuquerque. But we're not looking to enjoy a craft IPA next to a cement planter with decorative grasses in the southwestern modern style. No sir! We are here to pay homage. We are pilgrims. Louie's decor is traditional, the air conditioning is excellent, and the atmosphere is friendly and relaxed.

"The Guy for This" features Mike nursing his sorrows at Louie's. At real life Louie's, you would be left in peace to do this very thing. The pub you see on-camera is very similar to the pub in person, give or take a few details—the chairs have been switched out, but the tables remain the same. The real pub serves up wings, nachos, and the like, though we don't see our characters partake on-screen. Mike's coffee isn't a popular choice at the pub, but if you ask for one, take it black like our favorite hit man. Exterior signage is a little different—the show added a larger sign to the side of the pub. A friendly reminder to those who may wish to capture their trip on a phone camera or a point and shoot: The bar will not be lit by head gaffer Steve Litecky's team. Nor will the image be shot by cinematographer Marshall Addams as it was last time we saw Louie's on-screen. You're just going to end up with a very different look. And yes, even if you layer the photo with a bunch of filters . . . same story.

You may notice the on-camera beer pulls are different, so as not to infringe on brewers' trademarks. The script of *Better Call Saul*'s "Coushatta" makes a feature of German beer, but the brews working in the background have been switched out by the props department. As some of you may know, this is standard practice on TV shows so the production doesn't get dinged with hefty licensing fees. However, there are exceptions, and one of them is in this very bar in *Breaking Bad*. In "Thirty-Eight Snub," Walt orders a real-life beer, a "Fat Tire, draft" to be exact. It would be unreasonable to tell you that beer is always going to be on draft at Louie's, but why not look out for it? The pub's real draft list is expansive (twenty-four beers), with many local favorites.

Keep it simple with a local draft at this friendly pub. Sit at the left corner of the bar in homage to Mike.

LOYOLA'S FAMILY RESTAURANT $$

4500 Central Ave. SE, Albuquerque, 87108
(505) 268-6478
loyolasfamilyrestaurant.com
Tuesday–Saturday, 6:00 a.m.–2:00 p.m.

BB s4.e5, "Shotgun," August 14, 2011
BB s5.e2, "Madrigal," July 22, 2012
BCS s1.e1, "Uno," February 8, 2015
BCS s1.e5, "Alpine Shepherd Boy," March 2, 2015
BCS s2.e5, "Rebecca," March 14, 2016
BCS s2.e9, "Nailed," April 11, 2016
BCS s3.e4, "Sabrosito," May 1, 2017
BCS s4.e3, "Something Beautiful," August 20, 2018
BCS s4.e4, "Talk," August 27, 2018

This restaurant is named after its founder, Loyola Baca. Today her daughter Sarah Cordova is the owner and proprietor.[8] Before we take a deeper dive into this location, please remember it closes early. So go early! The reason I point this out is because we are introduced

FIGURE 32. At Loyola's Family Restaurant, Betsy and Craig Kettleman discuss whether they should sign a letter of engagement with Jimmy, after Craig has been charged with embezzlement, *BCS* s1.1, "Uno" (2015). Courtesy of Sony Pictures Television.

FIGURE 33. Loyola's exterior sign, 2022. Courtesy of Aimee Macpherson.

FIGURE 34. Loyola's coffee mug, 2022. Courtesy of Aimee Macpherson.

to the restaurant at night, specifically in *Breaking Bad*'s "Shotgun" episode, when Mike kindly offers Jesse the dinner he ordered for himself to help Jesse through a drug withdrawal. You are not going to get inside this place at night for a cup of black coffee, Mike style. But if you insist on going after dark, you could stand outside in an homage to Gus and Jesse's interaction in that same episode.

In the *Breaking Bad* and *Better Call Saul* universe, we Mike frequent Loyola's to grab a bite to eat and also hold several business meetings. Mike doesn't wear his heart on his sleeve at Loyola's—this is a place for pitching deals, deflecting crooked propositions, and getting a bite in relative safety. All the feels show up at Louie's Pub and Grill.

But Loyola's is not exclusively patronized by Mike. The first time we see Loyola's in *Better Call Saul* is with Jimmy McGill in "Uno." He's talking business (for want of a better phrase) with those lovable all-American parents Betsy Kettleman (Julie Ann Emery) and Craig Kettleman (Jeremy Shamos). Jimmy doesn't encroach on Mike's turf. Jimmy and the Kettlemans sit at the brown corner booth, close to the hot-air balloon mural, and all three have coffee mugs in front of them. Jimmy only crosses over to the side of the green booths when he is there to see Mike. After this reintroduction to Loyola's, the restaurant is featured many times in *Better Call Saul*, and it is still one of the few places that is virtually unaltered from the *Breaking Bad* days. Fran the waitress (Debrianna Mansini) works at the restaurant in both *Breaking Bad* and *Better Call Saul*, providing another layer of visual continuity between the two shows.

Loyola's will pretty much look just like it does on-screen, right down to the mugs and dinner plates (although there will not be anyone standing there with a reflector to help the light bounce off your beautiful face). Mike's booth is usually second down from the green corner booth; in the *Better Call Saul* episode "Nailed," he sits one down from that corner booth. Sometimes he faces the door, but not always because he is Mike and he can do what he wants. Drink in the leatherette illuminated by ceramic drop-down chain lights featuring hand-painted roadrunners and yuccas. This is an alternative aesthetic of Route 66 culture, a calmer one. The restaurant features original fixtures without the Day-Glo kitsch of a restored malt diner. Sure, you can get yummy fresh pie à la mode here, but there's no jukebox or Elvis Presley memorabilia. The floor is plain carpet, softening the footfall of busy diners, and the murals are painted in muted colors. Outside is a mural of a policeman with an old-time police helmet (custodian style), complete with an octagonal American-style stop sign above him that reads, "C'mon In."

There was a steady stream of customers when I walked into Loyola's after dropping my kid off at day care. As soon as I sat down, I overheard the waitstaff addressing several customers by their first names: "Good morning, Richard," "How you doing, Ms. Linda?" A bouquet of fresh flowers at the cashier's desk was remarked on by a few customers as unusual. This place is clearly home to many regulars. The coffee is served black in a modestly sized mug. My waitress had been working at Loyola's since the *Breaking Bad* days. I ordered huevos rancheros with two over-easy eggs, corn tortillas on the bottom, and green chile (because it was the spicier option that day). The pinto beans had a tortilla chip for garnish, sticking upright at the center. Both red and green chile is made from scratch in the kitchen; the spiciness depends on the chiles available. The potatoes are parboiled, then fried to give the home fries their comforting "gimme more" texture.

In *Breaking Bad*'s "Shotgun," it looks like Mike orders meat loaf smothered in gravy, with a side of corn. Loyola's currently doesn't have meat loaf on the menu, but under "House Suggestions" they offer a roast beef dinner smothered in gravy. The entrées are served with soup or mixed green salad, vegetables, and "choice of potato." For a little extra, you can add home fries (under two dollars last time I checked). The veggie sides rotate daily. So, depending on the season of your trip, you may or may not strike it lucky with corn on the cob. In the *Better Call Saul* episode "Rebecca," it looks like Mike partakes in two eggs sunny-side up; bacon; and hash browns with black coffee. For this meal, I'd suggest ordering from the section of the menu dubbed "The Usual." Coincidentally, in *Better Call Saul*'s "Nailed," Fran asks Mike, "Usual?" in reference to his breakfast order. The breakfast dish doesn't have a name, but it is listed as two eggs, home fries, and choice of bacon, sausage patty or link, ham, or chorizo. The menu specifically asks for no substitutions.

To replicate Mike's breakfast on *Better Call Saul*, order the first dish under "The Usual" section of the menu, plus a mug of black coffee.

NOTES

1. Jessica Dyer, "Losing an Institution," *Albuquerque Journal*, November 21, 2014.

2. The Last Supper, "Recreating Walter White's Last Meal of Hash Browns, Bacon & Eggs," April 19, 2021, YouTube video, 6:15, https://www.youtube.com/watch?v=BVrCL2M1O9U&ab_channel=TheLastSupper.

3. Damon Scott, "Longtime UNM-Area Denny's to Close," *Business Journal*, November 20, 2014, https://www.bizjournals.com/albuquerque/news/2014/11/20/longtime-unm-area-denny-s-to-close.html.

4. Wim Wenders, *Written in the West, Revisited* (New York: Distributed Art Publishers, 2015), 23.

5. Wenders, *Written in the West*, 2, 3.

6. Denny's, "Menu: Signature Breakfasts," accessed March 31, 2022, https://www.dennys.com/location/dennys-6214/menu/signature-breakfasts.

7. Yelp, Louie's Pub & Grill, accessed March 27, 2022, https://www.yelp.com/biz/louies-pub-and-grill-albuquerque?start=10.

8. Loyola's Family Restaurant, "About Us," accessed March 16, 2022, http://www.loyolasfamilyrestaurant.com/.

PEREA'S NEW MEXICAN RESTAURANT $

Shooting location (permanently closed)
9901 Central Ave. NE, Albuquerque, 87123
New location

1140 Juan Tabo Blvd. NE, Albuquerque, 87112
(505) 293-0157
facebook.com/people/Pereas-New-Mexican-Restaurant/100095816640376
Tuesday–Saturday, 7:00 a.m.–1:30 p.m.

BB s5.e10, "Buried," August 18, 2013

Perea's has moved since *Breaking Bad* used the restaurant to shoot a scene in season 5's "Buried." The location used in the show is now a day care center.[1] Please don't request to look around the day care—just go to Perea's new location on Juan Tabo. It is budget friendly, so you can go ALL OUT on classic New Mexican dishes.

Skyler and Hank have a fraught meeting at this restaurant. The setting of Perea's is another excellent use of a welcoming neighborhood breakfast joint. The quiet, low-key background provides an aching contrast to Hank's agenda: to try to get Skyler to identify her husband as the criminal Heisenberg. The folks in this restaurant are a world away from the drama and tension that fill Skyler's and Hank's lives, and it really shows. When Skyler shakes off Hank's grip and asks him "Am I under arrest?," we move to a wide shot and see the scene as though we're a patron at the diner too. It looks like a man is harassing a respectable-looking woman and she walks out on him to avoid further intimidation tactics. Of course, Hank and Skyler's relationship is a little bit more complex than that, but the public forum of the diner helps us look afresh at the changing power dynamic between these two characters.

On-screen you see the two at a cream vinyl booth with a window looking out onto an unremarkable view of Central Avenue, showcasing a few parked cars and some prefab homes. (There is no hint of the nighttime neon of Central's alter ego, Route 66, which gets

FIGURE 35. At Perea's New Mexican Restaurant, Hank tries to coerce Skyler into recording a confession, *BB* s5.e10, "Buried" (2013). Courtesy of Sony Pictures Television.

its time to shine in Chuck's stressful walk to a pay phone in *Better Call Saul* season 3, episode 6, "Off Brand.") Much like Central Avenue, both characters are doing their damnedest to act normal. As Hank tries to interrogate Skyler, two brown diner coffee mugs are on the table in front of them, and they speak in low tones. Ceramic light fixtures hang above the booths, framing diners below as they go about the ordinary business of eating at a family restaurant. Perea's new location looks different. For one, it has tables and chairs instead of the vinyl booths. But it still oozes authenticity. The brick floor, regional decor like paintings of adobe buildings, and wooden chile *ristras* all add to the charm. A chile ristra is a garland of dried New Mexican chiles threaded together with straw. It is to New Mexico what a white garlic wreath is to France. Ristras are brittle and deep red in color. The ones made of fresh chiles are dried in the sun.

Perea's serves a variety of authentic New Mexican dishes, but you can also try some Tex-Mex classics here, such as the chimichanga plate (a deep-fried burrito with all the fixings).

CAFE 66 NEW MEXICAN RESTAURANT $

a.k.a. somewhere on the freeway in Arizona
9200 Central Ave. SW, Albuquerque, 87121
(505) 974-5645
Sunday–Saturday, 7:00 a.m.–3:00 p.m.

BB s5.e11, "Confessions," August 25, 2013

You can drive to Cafe 66 (no acute accent on the "e") via Central Avenue, a.k.a. historic Route 66. This road eventually links up with I-40. Central Avenue SW is still lined with plenty of small neon signs advertising motels, palm reading, and auto repair. Some are retro and some are actual vintage; it feels like the older ones were preserved just because nobody felt like removing them. (On the way to Cafe 66, you will pass Westward Ho! Motel, located at Central Avenue SW and Seventy-Fifth Street. This motel was a location featured in *Better Call Saul* season 4, episode 4, "Talk." The empty buildings on this lot portrayed a hub for the Espinosa Gang and a cornerstone for action in the episode. Westward Ho! is easy to spot from the road because of the large green neon saguaro cactus sign outside.)

From the road, you first notice the side of the Cafe 66 building.

FIGURE 36. Cafe 66 New Mexican restaurant, as the Arizona diner exterior, BB s5.e11, "Confessions" (2013). Courtesy of Sony Pictures Television.

FIGURE 37. Cafe 66 interior, 2023. Courtesy of Aimee Macpherson.

FIGURE 38. Cafe 66 Cinnamon Toast, 2023. Courtesy of Aimee Macpherson.

It's got a bright-yellow wall painted with a black-and-white Route 66 badge. I pulled into the dirt lot and parked opposite the mural. It's the same mural we see behind Todd Alquist (Jesse Plemons) in the *Breaking Bad* episode "Confessions," when Todd steps outside the café to call Walt and leaves a voicemail. An oversized, bright-red neon sign that reads "CAFE" marks the front of the small diner's modest exterior. The sign stands over the edge of the roof above the windows. A low cinder block wall in front of the building separates the café from the dirt lot in front of it. To the left of the café is a well-maintained mobile home. Behind it is a Penske Truck Rental facility. In front is desert scrub scattered with debris from the road. I narrowly avoid stepping on a large fire ant nest as I walk toward the restaurant.

I enter the café through the door behind the mural, the same one Todd uses to reenter after calling Walt. Back inside at his table, Todd recounts to his uncle, the neo-Nazi gang leader Jack Welker, and Jack's associate Kenny (Kevin Rankin) just how brilliantly the train heist went. True to Todd, he omits the little detail about the homicide. Story-wise the scene is set in Arizona. Jack, Todd, and Kenny are driving back to New Mexico after murdering Declan (Louis Ferreira) and company. The trio leave their unfinished meal, pay the check, and hit the road.

Unsurprisingly, the café does not make a big fuss of the scene's location. Cafe 66, with its unironic Americana decor and patriotic clientele, are not interested in talking to you about Todd's breakfast. The table featured on the show is the fourth booth on the left by the window. There is a small framed picture of the characters hanging from a window panel above the booth with "Breaking Bad" printed in black lettering at the bottom of the image. By contrast, to the right of the restaurant, a large framed photo rests above the corner booth depicting the exterior of the café in extensive set dressing. Red font at the top of the picture reads "Movie NEW YEAR with Tom Hanks filmed at Cafe 66." I believe this wound up being the film *Bios* (2019).

Since the table in question was occupied by a couple eating hearty breakfasts, I went to the right of the restaurant. The dining booths are wrapped in deep-red, studded leatherette upholstery with rips patched over in duct tape. Vintage wallpaper on the back wall depicts small groups of trees and deer. Mounted on the wallpaper are photographs of local members of the US Army and a certificate of appreciation from Ladera US Army Recruiting Center.

The café's decor is pure Americana in the same vein as Loyola's. It is not retro imitation but vintage. The worn booth seats are a testament to the historic credentials of this eatery. The wood-varnished swing door to the kitchen is painted with a large roadrunner. At the bar top sat an older man and a woman, both wearing white aprons.

A waitress leaned over to them behind the counter, and in Spanish they talked through the orders on her notepad.

In this episode of *Breaking Bad*, it's hard to see what Todd and gang ordered, but coffee is certainly on the table. I sat down and was brought coffee and a menu right away. It came in a small D-ring mug, alongside a little saucer with a spoon resting on it. A little bowl of "long life" milk (milk that's been processed at an ultrahigh temperature) pods was placed next to the coffee. I cracked open one of the milk pods, added it to the coffee, and took a sip. It was piping hot and tasted strong. From the breakfast menu, wrapped in clear vinyl and decorated with clip art, I ordered Huevos a la Mexicana. The menu said it came with two scrambled eggs, but I reckon there must have been at least three on my plate. Mixed into the scramble were square cuts of jalapeño, tomato, and white onion. It was served with hash browns, crispy on the outside and soft on the inside. Served hot, it was a delicious and straightforward breakfast. I couldn't resist ordering a side of Cinnamon Toast from the "Toast and Rolls" section of the menu. Two small squares of sliced whole wheat cut on the diagonal, covered in melted butter, and sprinkled with cinnamon sugar appeared before me. The toast was served on a little plate that almost fit into the palm of my hand. Sidenote: Cafe 66 does not have a website, but the 66 Diner does. It is also on Central. Take care to check whether you're headed to Cafe 66 on Central Avenue *SW* or 66 Diner on Central Avenue *NE*.

Go to Cafe 66 for comforting diner food. The substantial breakfasts are available all day. Don't forget to round off the meal with a hot coffee and some Cinnamon Toast.

GARDUÑO'S OF MEXICO $$$

Shooting location (permanently closed)
Winrock Town Center, 2100 Louisiana Blvd., Albuquerque, 87110
Reviewed location

Hotel Albuquerque at Old Town, 800 Rio Grande Blvd. NW, 87104
(505) 222-8766
hotelabq.com/eat_drink/gardunos
Sunday–Saturday, 7:00 a.m.–11:00 p.m.

BB s5.e11, "Confessions," August 25, 2013

Breaking Bad filmed at a Garduño's located in Albuquerque's Winrock Town Center for "Confessions." The scene opens with a wide shot: Walt and Skyler sitting in silence, glum faced at the center of a busy restaurant, with colorful hats and sunflowers behind them. The convivial atmosphere and colorful decor are at total odds with the couple's somber vibe and neutral clothing. They are waiting for Hank and Marie, who arrive looking equally somber. Walt doesn't beat around the bush and immediately asks Hank and Marie to leave

FIGURE 39. Skyler and Walt have a tense exchange with Marie and Hank at Garduño's of Mexico, *BB* s5.e11, "Confessions" (2013). Courtesy of Sony Pictures Television.

FIGURE 40. Garduño's Nachos Tradicionales and a Silver Coin Margarita, 2022. Courtesy of Aimee Macpherson.

their children out of Hank's new investigation at work—which aims to arrest Walt for cooking and distributing meth under the alias Heisenberg. Walt insists there is "nothing to confess" and Hank should think of how this will affect Walt Jr. Hank does not back down and insists he's going after an arrest.

As anticipated, the conversation is unproductive and neither side concedes ground. You'd be fair in thinking that the dramatic kicker is Marie telling Walt to just "go kill himself." And while that line certainly packs a punch, the real drama is when Walt puts down a DVD in a clear-blue plastic case on the table in front of Hank. Walt says nothing about the content. He and Skyler leave in silence. We already know that Walt recorded a confession, and we are led to assume that's on the DVD. In the next scene, we watch the recording with Hank and Marie. Turns out the confession isn't a confession at all—it's blackmail. The goal of the recording by Walt is to show Hank he can and will ruin both Hank's credibility and his career if Hank continues to try to build an investigation against Walt.

The Garduño's used for this episode closed in July 2021.[2] The restaurant franchise was founded in Albuquerque in 1981 by Dave Garduño.[3] Today you can still visit Garduño's at their locations inside Hotel Albuquerque, at the Cottonwood Mall (10031 Coors Blvd. NW, Albuquerque, 87114), and at the Nativo Lodge (6000 Pan American Fwy. NE, Albuquerque, 87109).

I chose to visit the restaurant located in Hotel Albuquerque, and although this Garduño's is not the original filming location, it conveys much of the jovial atmosphere and colorful decor we see on-screen. As the restaurant's slogan goes, "Always fresh, always a fiesta!" You enter the restaurant by walking through the main lobby of the hotel and making a sharp left turn. I visited on a hot summer afternoon. Walking toward Hotel Albuquerque's main entrance, the temperature was working its way to a hundred degrees, and the sky above was a brilliant, cloudless blue. Once I pulled open the door (hot to the touch), air conditioning hitting the lobby's cool tile floor made the inside inviting and restorative. The outside of the restaurant is marked with an oval-style opening in the wall, flanked by cast-iron candelabras. The Garduño's logo in red and yellow is painted over the opening. To the left I saw a floor manager behind a heavy carved wood lectern. Inside the restaurant are colorful murals painted on glass windows, light fixtures made with New Mexico tin-work, a large bar, and a yellow ceiling with blue diamond patterns. At the table are leather-embossed place mats and bright-blue cloth napkins. The dining chairs are wood, carved in the Spanish colonial style with a red cushion.

Walt, Skyler, Hank, and Marie don't order anything in this scene, despite valiant efforts by their server, Trent (Guy Wilson). That means you can order whatever you fancy when you visit today. Follow Trent's suggestions and start with a margarita and the guac. They no longer make it at the table like Trent mentions. However, it's still fresh and made to order. I ordered the Nachos Tradicionales and a Silver Coin Margarita. The cocktail menu is extensive. I counted eleven margaritas, with flavors ranging from prickly pear or jalapeño to specialty tequila like the Don Julio 1942. My margarita arrived first, in a clear bubble glass with a chunky blue rim, encrusted with salt. I disregarded the dainty black plastic straws that came inside the beverage and took a swig from the rim. Made with Espolón Silver tequila, Patrón Citrónge Orange, fresh-pressed lime juice, and agave nectar, the Silver Coin Margarita is a refreshing and zesty classic. The glass is substantial, and it takes a few practices to pick it up and set it down without wobbling the cloudy, pale-green beverage inside. It's a good thing the nachos arrived swiftly after the cocktail. Piled high on a wide plate, the dish is warm and comforting, the perfect contrast to a margarita. There's nothing unexpected in the Nachos Tradicionales—the name gives everything away—and that means you get to indulge in a luxurious take on a familiar appetizer. Warm corn chips smothered with melty shredded cheese rest over a large helping of beans, guacamole, jalapeños, tomatoes, and sour cream. I ordered my guac and sour cream on the side, and I found the dish was several inches tall, generous enough to serve as a snack for at least two hungry people.

Start with a margarita and the guac. For a heavyweight snack, order the Nachos Tradicionales with *machaca* (dried spiced beef originally from northern Mexico that texture-wise lands somewhere between ground beef and bacon).

PONDEROSA FAMILY RESTAURANT & GRILL

a.k.a. bar in the fictional Crawford County
Shooting location (permanently closed)
10676 NM 14/337 Tijeras, NM, 87059

BB s5.e15, "Granite State," September 22, 2013

This location served as the New Hampshire bar where Mr. Lambert (Walt's pseudonym) orders the final neat Dimple Pinch in *Breaking Bad*'s penultimate episode. Today the restaurant is closed, and probably for good, so you can't glimpse the wood-paneled interior with quaint rustic decor. On-screen, you can see behind Walt the logo of New Hampshire's Smuttynose Brewing Co. The logo for this real-life craft beer business features a distinctive drawing of a harbor seal.

FIGURE 41. Whiskey on the bar at Ponderosa Family Restaurant & Grill (as a bar in New Hampshire), *BB* s5.e15, "Granite State" (2013). Courtesy of Sony Pictures Television.

THE GROVE CAFE & MARKET $$

600 Central Ave. SE, Ste. A., Albuquerque, 87102
(505) 248-9800
thegrovecafemarket.com
Tuesday–Sunday, 8:00 a.m.–2:00 p.m.

BB s5.e16, "Felina," September 29, 2013

Many TV critics hail "Felina" as one of the all-time greatest series finales in television history. This episode packs many punches, and right up there is the one to Lydia Rodarte-Quayle (Laura Fraser). Her scene at the Grove is still a knockout to watch.

Walt poisons Lydia's tea with ricin by filling a packet of stevia with the deadly poison. He's already at the café when she arrives, and she sits at the table where they usually met to do business. He swapped out one of the packets on the table before she arrived, betting she would sit at her regular spot. We don't see her die on-screen, but we are given a hint it's unlikely she will survive. Walt's simple but risky plan relied on her being a creature of habit. He's been dreaming of a way to kill off Lydia with ricin for a long time (see *Breaking Bad* s5.e8, "Gliding Over All") but just hadn't built up the nerve to do it until the

FIGURE 42. Stevia in Lydia's tea at the Grove Cafe & Market, *BB* s5.e16, "Felina" (2013). Courtesy of Sony Pictures Television.

FIGURE 43. Stevia at the Grove, 2023. Courtesy of Aimee Macpherson.

FIGURE 44. Lydia's regular table at the Grove, 2023. Courtesy of Aimee Macpherson.

season finale. Lydia has been at the Grove plotting ways to kill Walt (see *Breaking Bad* s5.e15, "Granite State," the episode before the finale). However, Walt outpaces her, delivering her the deadly blow first.

Lydia's signature drink is chamomile tea with soy milk and stevia. The *Wrap* quotes Vince Gilligan saying he puts milk in all kinds of tea, chamomile included, and his thinking behind Lydia's drink was that soy just sounded a bit healthier than regular milk.[4] I guess we have it straight from the source that her unusual choice of hot beverage is not a secret dig at yuppie, hot-beverage culture that was springing up around the time of filming.

The Grove does offer chamomile tea, but it's mixed with other herbs. They do not sell soy milk; cow milk alternatives on the menu are coconut, almond, and oat. The café recently updated their exterior seating layout to increase their capacity for outdoor dining. However, the furniture and style of the café interior remain very similar to that featured on the show. Unlike Twisters in the South Valley, however, the café does not have a mural on the wall to help TV fans find the spot where the characters sat. You'll just have to use your powers of recall (or download the episode onto your phone) to get the right seat. When I visited, one of the staff members asked if I was looking for "the table." He didn't elaborate, but we both knew what he was talking about. I said yes and he happily pointed me in the right direction. He said he'd been working at the Grove for eleven years and he still encounters people looking for Lydia's seat. The mugs are either a C ring or a wide cup and saucer. Both are white, unlike the colorful mug we see in the show.

In real life, it's positively mandatory to stop here for coffees on early-morning location scouts. Their lunches have the magic factor that make crew happy, and the sweet treats are a perfect afternoon pick-me-up. This café works on many levels in the *Breaking Bad* universe. It's a scene on-camera, it's a place that is loved by cast and crew, and it's got a loyal following of Albuquerque residents who visit the eatery regularly, without ever even thinking about the legendary TV moment filmed inside.

Part of what many people love about the Grove is their delicious and consistent menu built from locally sourced ingredients. The restaurant usually offers a seasonal soup, salad, and main dish, but for those of us who are creatures of habit, like Lydia, you can order the rest of the menu by heart.

Order a vanilla latte and the pancakes. The stevia is on the condiments counter to the left of the main entrance in a white ceramic container.

NOTES

1. Childcare Center, "Avengers Learning Center," accessed March 18, 2022, https://childcarecenter.us/provider_detail/avengers-learning-center-ld-albuquerque-nm.

2. “Uptown Garduño’s to Close,” KRQE, June 22, 2021, https://www.krqe.com/news/business/uptown-gardunos-to-close/.

3. Garduño’s of Mexico, “About Us,” http://gardunosrestaurants.com/about-us/.

4. Tony Maglio, “‘Breaking Bad’ Creator Vince Gilligan Finally Explains Why Lydia Took Her Tea Like That,” the *Wrap*, January 25, 2018, https://www.thewrap.com/breaking-bad-vince-gilligan-lydia-chamomile-tea-soy-milk-stevia.

Better Call Saul

CINNABON $

Shooting location (permanently closed)
Cottonwood Mall, 10000 Coors Byp. NW, Albuquerque, 87114
Reviewed location

Coronado Center, 6600 Menaul Blvd. NE, Ste. 5, Albuquerque, 87110
(505) 881-8044
locations.cinnabon.com/nm/albuquerque/6600-menaul-blvd-ne
Sunday, 11:00 a.m.–6:00 p.m.
Monday–Saturday, 11:00 a.m.–8:00 p.m.

BCS s1.e1, "Uno," February 8, 2015
BCS s2.e1, "Switch," February 16, 2016
BCS s3.e1, "Mabel," April 10, 2017
BCS s4.e1, "Smoke," August 6, 2018
BCS s5.e1, "Magic Man," February 23, 2020
BCS s6.e10, "Nippy," July 25, 2022
BCS s6.e11, "Breaking Bad," August 1, 2022

Oh, Cinnabon, where to begin? "Life needs frosting," of course! This baked-goods chain is first mentioned in the *Breaking Bad* universe in

FIGURE 45. Cinnabon interior, *BCS* s1.e1, "Uno" (2015). Courtesy of Sony Pictures Television.

FIGURE 46. A Cinnabon Classic Roll, 2022. Courtesy of Aimee Macpherson.

Breaking Bad penultimate episode, "Granite State," when Saul Goodman explains his prospects to Walter White: "If I'm lucky, a month from now, best case scenario, I'm managing a Cinnabon in Omaha." That episode was written and directed by Peter Gould, who would go on to be the showrunner of *Better Call Saul* two years later. Cut to *Better Call Saul*'s premier, "Uno," and we finally get to see with our own eyes proof that Saul wrangled the best-case scenario.

The location we see in *Better Call Saul* was shot in the real Cinnabon bakery at Cottonwood Mall, located in Albuquerque, not Nebraska. The location closed after season 4, but the production as able to continue filming there for season 5. The location was briefly home to a Crepes & Waffles café. It is now available for lease, which means it's not accessible to the general public. The general architecture of the mall remains identical to that featured on *Better Call Saul*. Dillard's clothing store and Nail Pro manicures are two businesses at this location that are featured on-screen. The bench where Gene (formerly Saul, formerly Jimmy) sits to have lunch in season 5's "Magic Man," which is recognized by Jeff the cab driver (played by Don Harvey in seasons 4 and 5), is part of the property on the second floor of the mall.

Props to Cinnabon for permitting the show to use their real company name. Regarding the franchise's namesake baked goods, those sugary buns are served with melty frosting seeping into the crevices of cinnamon-y dough, warm from the oven. At two Cinnabon locations in town, you can order your own just like the ones you see Gene make. I visited the franchise at the Coronado Center (the other location is at the Flying J Travel Center, 991 Avalon Rd. NW, Albuquerque, 87121). The bakery has a narrow presence on the second level of the mall. You can smell the cinnamon before you see the display counter, packed full of rolls. There is a mixer on display much like the one at Gene's franchise, and tables and chairs are laid out in front of the counter. The business does swift trade; it's a stressful place to sit because you are in a busy entryway to the mall with plenty of customers passing in and out of the building.

Many customers choose to eat their baked goods on the go. I observed a pro eating several MiniBons on the move while pushing a stroller. He was able to use the stroller handle to balance the aquamarine cardboard CinnaPack in one hand, leaving the other hand free to pop the little rolls in his mouth. If you are an amateur like me, you will need to copy Frank Danielsen (Jim O'Heir), the security guard Gene wins over with a daily dose of the Classic Roll in "Nippy," and eat this baby sitting down with a knife and fork. It should be warm. The real-life rolls have much less frosting than the ones featured on Frank's plate. On my roll, the frosting looked more like a glaze than white paint. I reckon you'd have to order several extra portions of frosting (don't worry, they are available at the bakery) to achieve the same look.

You can order the Classic Roll, but they also have smaller offerings like the MiniBon roll or BonBites if you're just looking for a taste of what you've seen Gene handling for six consecutive seasons of *Better Call Saul*. The bakery also serves signature drinks, such as Chillattas, but it may be more on brand for Gene Takovic disciples to chase down that bun with a simple hot black coffee. Additionally, the show makes a point of hiring and rehiring a real-life Cinnabon employee to be featured at work alongside Gene. On IMDb Raquel Pino has a credit as Cinnabon Employee #2 from 2015. But starting in 2016, she got an actor's credit as Raquel on the show through 2020.[1]

No other show dedicates such award-winning cinematography to fast-food preparation. Fast-food end products are certainly revered in other productions, like the famous Royale with cheese in

Pulp Fiction (1994) or the Krusty Burger from *The Simpsons*. But the sophisticated way in which fast-food franchises are portrayed in *Breaking Bad* and *Better Call Saul* really sets the show apart. Here Cinnabon isn't some evil harbinger of white-sugar highs—it's a sanctuary, albeit a precarious one, for our charismatic mail room clerk, con man, ex-attorney, cell phone salesman, and all-around outsider Gene Takovic, I mean Saul Goodman, oh wait, really he's Jimmy McGill . . . or is he? Let's get back to the buns.

There is a lovingly detailed short documentary from 2018 called *Gene of Omaha*, which you can find in the *Better Call Saul* season 3 DVD extras, that goes into the detail of creating that little slice of Omaha. Check it out to find out more straight from the cast and crew about how to make a closed mall look open during filming hours. At 6:30 a.m., obviously the shops are closed, but those early hours create an opportunity for a more controlled environment essential for filming. The documentary also peeps into the labor-intensive craft of time lapses and in-camera stunts that help build this show's unique style.

To visit the original Cinnabon location, head to the Cottonwood Mall. For an actual Cinnabon bun, head to the Coronado Center.

CAFÉ LUSH

$

700 Tijeras Ave. NW, Albuquerque, 87102
(505) 508-0164
cafelushabq.com
Monday–Friday, 7:00 a.m.–1:30 p.m.
Saturday, 8:00 a.m.–1:00 p.m.

BCS s1.e1, "Uno," February 8, 2015

If we're getting technical, the first episode of *Better Call Saul* features the intersection at Tijeras Avenue NW and Seventh Street NW. This is where Café Lush is located. The café's exterior is featured clearly in the background of the scene where we see Jimmy in action for the first time. We don't have any on-screen action inside the café or closeup shots of their food.

Jimmy hires two skateboarders and budding con artists, who are near-identical brothers Cal Lindholm (Daniel Spenser Levine) and Lars Lindholm (Steven Levine) (who are real-life twins), to perform a scam on a specific car at the intersection outside Café Lush. Their stunt involves one brother falling off a skateboard as if struck by a car, while the other brother films the incident on a camcorder. The

FIGURE 47. The Lindholm twins face Café Lush, ready to execute their scam, *BCS* s1.e1, "Uno" (2015). Courtesy of Sony Pictures Television.

FIGURE 48. Café Lush Breakfast Pizza, 2022. Courtesy of Aimee Macpherson.

brothers were supposed to scam the Kettlemans' 1988 Mercury Sable but instead they hit a 1993 Ford Taurus. Although this car looks very similar to the Kettlemans', the driver is not Betsy Kettleman but Abuelita, Tuco Salamanca's grandmother (Miriam Colon).

Café Lush was opened in 2011 by husband-and-wife team Thomas Docherty and Sandy Gregory, and they still run the show.[2] Sandy was even featured as an extra in that first episode of *Better Call Saul*, seated outside her café.[3] The real restaurant has metal seats with parasols lined up outside; there are a few small tables inside. It is in Albuquerque's downtown, near St. Mary's Catholic School and on the edge of Albuquerque's Fourth Ward Historic Protection Overlay Zone. The area has a variety of historic residential homes in various early twentieth-century styles.

A popular breakfast and lunch destination for locals, Café Lush has a quirky menu that emphasizes an eclectic mix of modern health foods. One regular, a lawyer with an office in the neighborhood, recommended I try the Breakfast Pizza. I sat outside on a bright afternoon and ordered one. The Breakfast Pizza is much more wholesome than the name suggests. A disc of shredded potato, sour cream, and scallions form the base. It had a warm salsa-style sauce with melty cheddar cheese, two eggs (over easy for me), shredded lettuce, diced tomato, and a warm tortilla on the side. I also had a tall glass of fresh orange juice. The sound of fellow diners and children from the nearby school gave the alfresco venue a neighborhood feel despite its location just a few blocks away from the Second Judicial District Court of Bernalillo County and the Albuquerque Convention Center.

Go for lunch and order the Quinoa Salad—dense and healthy ingredients like fresh mint, pepitas, carrots, dried cranberries, and organic greens make for a satisfying lunch, and the maple-mint dressing gives it a sweet twist. If you plan to walk the neighborhood, order a to-go latte topped with Lush Dust: cinnamon, cocoa, cardamom, and powdered sugar.

BAR UNO $$

a.k.a. Dearborn Cafe, Chicago
108 Second St. SW, Albuquerque, 87102
barunoabq.com
Monday–Sunday, 4:00 p.m.–1:30 a.m.

BCS s1.e4, "Hero," February 23, 2013

The doors to Wheelright bar are in a flashback at the start of "Hero." I believe it's the first time we hear Jimmy refer to himself as Saul Goodman on the show. His new pal Stevie (Kevin Weisman) is intoxicated and stumbles out of the bar. "Saul" on the other hand appears sober enough to drive—or pull off a scam. They find an opportunity to rob an unconscious man behind the bar. But of course, the unconscious man is actually Jimmy's friend Marco Pasternak (Mel Rodriguez). And they've scammed the scammer into swapping hard cash for a faux designer watch.

The Wheelright sign is actually attached to the Sunshine Building, currently not a restaurant or bar open to the public. Featured in

FIGURE 49. Bar Uno exterior, as Dearborn Cafe in Chicago, *BCS* s1.e4, "Hero" (2015). Courtesy of Sony Pictures Television.

a wide shot of Second Street, there is a closed diner called Dearborn Cafe next to the Wheelright. That café is actually Bar Uno, and you can head inside for a cocktail. It touts itself as Albuquerque's smallest bar, and a very dog-friendly little place it is too. Open from 4:00 p.m. until late, this neighborhood bar is perfect for your *apéro* hour before dinner. The cocktail menu has light, bittersweet classics like an americano or aperol spritz.

Sticking to the *Better Call Saul* theme, Bar Uno has a Moscow Mule (made with vodka) but also a Glasgow Mule (Scotch). Both use lime juice and Zia Ginger Ale, made by Zia Beverage, a New Mexico–based company making canned soda and tea. Zia Ginger Ale is made without corn syrup, using cane sugar, fresh-pressed ginger juice, red chile natural flavors, and lemon and lime juice. The Moscow Mule here is spicy, with enough acidity from the citrus to make sure ginger remains the main attraction.

Head to Bar Uno for apéro hour—now is the chance to switch up your mule from Moscow to Glasgow.

VINTAGE 423 $$$

8000 Paseo del Norte NE, Ste. A1, Albuquerque, 87122
(505) 821-1918
vintage-423.com
Sunday–Thursday, 11:00 a.m.–12:00 a.m.
Friday–Saturday, 11:00 a.m.–2:00 a.m.

BCS s1.e2, "Mijo," February 9, 2015
BCS s2.e1, "Switch," February 15, 2016
BCS s3.e7, "Expenses," May 22, 2017

Time for a vibe shift! Vintage 423 is all about texture: plush velvet, leather, an alabaster bar top, water features . . . I could go on. The service is excellent, the drinks are ice cold, the food is served piping hot and in a timely fashion, the chairs are comfortable, and the lighting is flattering. If the corner of the famous alabaster bar where Jimmy sits (yes, it really does light up at night) is unavailable, you have plenty of options either outside on the patio which is well appointed with space heaters or inside lit by wavy pink light shades. The bar top is smooth and cool against the skin. The base is enveloped in what feels

FIGURE 50. Vintage 423 interior, *BCS* s2.e1, "Switch" (2016). Courtesy of Sony Pictures Television.

FIGURE 51. Virgin Moscow Mule at Vintage 423, 2022. Courtesy of Aimee Macpherson.

like pebbled black leather. The smooth, yellow leather-style bar chairs are extremely cushy and invite you take your time.

The chandelier above Jimmy "Mijo" is still in evidence at the bar. I don't currently see any breadsticks on the menu, so you'll have to use your own if you want to re-create the snap of one breaking, a trigger for Jimmy because it reminds him of broken bones—and anyway, this is probably an homage best done at home so as not to disturb the other customers. Honestly, the snap might get lost in the hubbub of the bar without a professional sound crew there to rig and amplify the sound for you.

Kicking off *Better Call Saul* season 2, Vintage 423 provides the backdrop for Jimmy and Kim to play a scam duet as "Viktor" and "Giselle" in "Switch." Poor old Ken (Kyle Bornheimer) plays right into their hands and they couldn't be more delighted. Happily for you, much of the actual restaurant decor was featured in camera, so you're really able to experience the look of the scenes here for yourself. And while Zafiro Añejo tequila is not a beverage available in the real world, at Vintage you really can order Rémy Martin Louis XIII that starts at a hundred dollars for a half-ounce pour. Cognac and tequila obviously taste very different, but there is a real-world extravagance to the price of this Remy Martin that ties it to the role Zafiro Añejo plays on-screen.

Ken is of course another Easter egg for *Breaking Bad* fans. He drives a 1996 BMW318i Cabrio that features a custom license plate that says, "Ken Wins." This reference is from way back in *Breaking Bad* season 1, episode 4, "Cancer Man," which aired in 2008. Ken Wins, the boorish wealth manager who appears in that episode, is still popping up for a feature in *Better Call Saul* season 2 eight years later! This is another example of the incredible detail that goes into building the continuity between these two shows.

By the time season 3 rolls around, Kim's appetite for rustling up another scam at the bar has cooled off. Both she and Jimmy talk about potential targets at the bar, but they don't follow through. At this point, Kim casts doubt on her previous enthusiasm for going along with Jimmy's more "creative" schemes, but it's hard to forget how much fun she had joining him in season 2.

Vintage 423 itself is both a bar and a restaurant with indoor and outdoor dining. The location has good views of the Sandia Mountains, and when the french windows onto the outside patio are open, the bar has an airy and refreshing feeling. The restaurant is equally popular for a late brunch as it is for an evening cocktail. Between the sizable appetizers and lunch and dinner menus, diners are left spoiled with choices. If you go for a late afternoon like Jimmy and Kim, order the shishito peppers roasted with sea salt and house-made spicy ponzu sauce to accompany your cocktail. Vintage has their list of staple cocktails, including the Lotus, the Aston Martin, the Cobra Cosmo, and the GT. The Lotus comes with Chopin vodka, Caravella Limoncello, fresh-squeezed lemon juice, and their Famous Lotus Button, which comes with an exciting warning: "Your taste buds will start tingling with a warm citrus pepper feeling. The tanginess moves to a slight numbness in the mouth for an experience you won't forget. *Limited supply.*" Their Famous Mules come in the classic copper mug, garnished with a fresh mint sprig. The food menu has many vintage twists on the classics, such as the standout lunch dish Dos Equis Beer Battered Fish and Chips, which comes with a jicama slaw, french fries, and traditional tartar sauce.

I visited Vintage in the early afternoon on a Friday, and it had a pleasant, relaxed atmosphere. The patio was already populated with well-heeled clientele ordering their lunch. I almost wish I'd brought a *New Yorker,* so I could hang out at the bar a bit longer. At the bar were a band of three friends, discussing their dogs' separation anxiety over a satisfying lunch—fish and chips, a burger, and a hearty sandwich. Two women behind me discussed natural birth while ordering cocktails. I decided to run with the *Better Call Saul* theme and get a Famous Mule; since I still had to collect my kid from day care, I made it a virgin cocktail. Honestly, I am still thinking about the chilled hammered copper mug perspiring on a neat black cocktail napkin. It was so cold, I almost got a brain freeze. The mug kind of hurt my hands to hold, but the ginger brought me back down to earth, and I managed not to slurp down the entire drink at once. The shishito peppers are excellent, and I think they work perfectly as a light but extremely flavorful side. The smoky grilled heat of the dish is powerful enough to compete with a cocktail but much lighter than fries, so it won't make you sleepy or fill you up before a main course.

Like many other bars and restaurants in Albuquerque, Vintage 423 is located in an unassuming mall, and other vendors currently include a FedEx Office, Integrity Firearms, and European Wax Center. The same mall also has a Flying Star Cafe, a local franchise that is more family friendly if you're traveling with kids.

Order a Famous Mule with a side of peppers. For a sit-down meal, don't sleep on the fish and chips.

TWO FOOLS TAVERN $$

a.k.a. McClure's, Philadelphia
3211 Central Ave. NE, Albuquerque, 87106
(505) 265-7447
2foolstavern.com
Sunday, 11:00 a.m.–4:00 p.m.
Monday–Thursday, 11:00 a.m.–10:00 p.m.
Friday–Saturday, 11:00 a.m.–11:00 p.m.

BCS s1.e6, "Five-O," March 9, 2015

McClure's in Philadelphia, the bar featured in "Five-O," is actually Two Fools Tavern in Albuquerque's Nob Hill. Although the Philadelphia bar only appears once, briefly in a flashback, it foreshadows Mike's weighty and emotional revelation to Stacey (Kelly Condon) about the death of Matt (the young version of whom is played by Nicholas Liam King), Stacey's husband and Mike's son—a cornerstone of Mike's MO in *Better Call Saul*. The encounter with cops Troy Hoffman (Lane Garrison) and Jack Fensky (Billy Malone) at the bar is another example of Mike duping both malevolent characters on the show and also us, his doting audience. It's not clear what Mike is drinking, or pretending to drink, in this scene, but if I were to take an educated guess, it's whiskey. And you're in luck, because the real Two Fools claims it has one of the largest selections of whiskeys in the Southwest.

The menu is full of classics like Scotch Eggs, but also has a few unusual items, like the Two Fools Irish Nachos, featuring homemade potato chips topped with cheddar, green chile, and beef cottage pie. The local favorite is their fish and chips, a gourmet take on the traditional, which offers two pieces of house ale–battered North Atlantic haddock.[4] The decor at Two Fools is a world away from the Southwest, with its dark interior, heavy wood , stained glass, and European–style trinkets. Unlike the McClure's it portrays on *Better Call Saul*, Two Fools is welcoming and family friendly. In happier times, it would seem quite fitting to see Mike order himself something from the bar here with a friend. It's as though the character of these locations has somehow managed to leak into their on-screen cameos, despite all the set dressing, lighting, and sophisticated camerawork that packages these locations to us viewers.

FIGURE 52. Two Fools Tavern interior, as McClure's in Philadelphia, *BCS* s1.e6, "Five-O" (2015). Courtesy of Sony Pictures Television.

The Irish pub has a nationwide appeal in North America, and Two Fools is no exception. Eateries come and go, but this place is a treasured establishment for Albuquerque locals. But what is the origin of this ye olde pub theme? (And no, I'm not talking about the tenth-century tavern in County Westmeath.[5]) I was surprised to discover that the Irish pub concept we know today is actually relatively new. It originates from a PR scheme cooked up by Guinness and the Irish Pub Company in the 1990s to sell beer.[6]

The episode featuring Two Fools received two primetime Emmy Award nominations: Gordon Smith for Outstanding Writing for a Drama Series and Kelley Dixon for Outstanding Single-Camera Picture Editing for a Drama Series. The episode was directed by Adam Bernstein, who first worked on *Breaking Bad* in 2008, directing season 1, episode 2, "Cat's in the Bag . . ." "Five-O" was the first of four episodes he directed on *Better Call Saul*. He directed eight episodes of *Breaking Bad*.

This tavern has an extensive selection of scotch and bourbon. For food, they have everything from a comforting snack like the Scotch Egg to something more substantial like the Liffey Chips (their version of fish and chips).

EDELWEISS AM RIO GRANDE $

a.k.a. Arno's, Cicero
4821 Menaul Blvd. NE, Albuquerque, 87110
(505) 888-4833
edelweissgac.org
Tuesday and Thursday (tentatively), 4:00 p.m.–8:00 p.m.
Wednesday and Friday, 4:00 p.m.–8:00 p.m.
Saturday, 12:00 p.m.–8:00 p.m.

BCS s1.e10, "Marco," April 6, 2015

This German American member club started in Albuquerque during the 1950s. It promotes friendship and community among German Americans living in the city. But you don't have to have family roots in Deutschland to enjoy a "bier" at the bar, since the club extends its hospitality to anyone wishing to visit.

A distinctive exterior to the club helps to sell that we're not in the 505 anymore. The nods to Bavarian culture in the faux timbers and coats of arms on the bar's exterior continue inside with a *Bauernstube*-style decor. Both the club interior and exterior are featured on the show as the setting for Arno's, a locals bar in Cicero, Illinois. We visit it twice in "Marco," at the end of the first season of *Better Call Saul*.

FIGURE 53. Jimmy walks toward Arno's bar in Cicero (Albuquerque's Edelweiss am Rio Grande), *BCS* s1.e10, "Marco" (2015). Courtesy of Sony Pictures Television.

In the teaser, the bar provides the backdrop for a flashback of Slippin' Jimmy telling Marco he's going to work in the mail room at his brother's firm. Marco isn't thrilled that Jimmy is going straight: "It's like watching Miles Davis give up the trumpet."

Back in the present, Jimmy's breakdown in the Albuquerque bingo hall prompts him to return to Arno's. And whom should he stumble into but his old pal and coconspirator Marco? Jimmy is seen holding a bottle of Old Style ("Chicago's beer") when he starts talking to Marco. This brand of beer may not be available at the club when you go there for a beverage, but I'm pretty sure they'll have a worthy stand-in available. For old time's sake, Marco and Jimmy scam a businessmen at Arno's. They convince him to buy "rare" half-dollar coin (the Kennedy coin) for $110, and their success in duping this sucker encourages them to go on a weeklong scamming spree.

The good times come to a halt at Marco's apartment when Sabrina (Amy Davidson), the woman he'd spent the night with, wakes up Jimmy with, "Hey! You are not Kevin Costner!" and Jimmy replies, "I was last night." This is another little Easter egg moment for the *Breaking Bad* fans. In "Abiquiu" (*BB* s3.e11), Jimmy tells Walt about pretending to be Kevin Costner to impress a woman: "It worked because I believed it."

The club genuinely has a neighborhood feel, and the setup is both unpretentious and welcoming. The doors are kept open by a group of diligent volunteers, making it a social club in the truest sense—it has the casual and authentic atmosphere of a tailgating party, but it's indoors. Edelweiss has reinstated many of the activities it put on hold during COVID-19. Check out the calendar on their website for an up-to-date list of what's available during your visit; often, there are dances and even a jazz night on the schedule. Prost!

Call ahead to check you're visiting during open hours. Order a bottled beer at the bar and toast to Marco.

NOTES

1. IMDb, s.v. "Raquel Pino," accessed March 16, 2022, https://www.imdb.com/name/nm7114591/.

2. Café Lush, home page, accessed March 18, 2022, http://www.cafelushabq.com/.

3. Ty Bannerman, "Better Call Lush," *Weekly Alibi*, February 5, 2015, https://alibi.com/food/48515/Better-Call-Lush.html.

4. Two Fools Tavern, "Menu," accessed March 28, 2022, https://www.2foolstavern.com/menu/.

5. Sean's Bar, "Sean's Bar History," accessed March 28, 2022, https://www.seansbar.ie/seans-bar-history.

6. Wikipedia, s.v. "Irish pub," last modified January 24, 2024, 17:02, https://en.wikipedia.org/wiki/Irish_pub.

HYATT REGENCY TAMAYA RESORT AND SPA $$$

1300 Tuyuna Trl., Santa Ana Pueblo, 87004
(505) 867-1234
hyatt.com/hyatt-regency/en-US/tamay-hyatt-regency-tamaya-resort-and-spa

BCS s2.e1, "Switch," February 15, 2016

Jimmy McGill kicks off act 2 of "Switch" with an outstanding performance in the Oxbow Pool at the Tamaya. I think my personal favorite prop here is the flip phone in a zip-up plastic bag that Jimmy keeps with him in the water. The pool establishes a great visual tension between the dysfunctional couple of Jimmy and Kim, reminding us of how impossibly mismatched they seem. Kim, in her polished office wear with a serious demeanor, is standing at the edge of the water looking down at Jimmy, who's bobbing about on his pool floatie, eating nachos as the New Mexico sunlight beats down on his exposed tummy. She mocks him—"So this is what a midlife crisis looks like"—but Jimmy's poker face has the upper hand. He's just being himself! Then hotel waiter approaches the pool and addresses Jimmy by a fake name. When they meet up at

FIGURE 54. Jimmy in the Oxbow Pool at Hyatt Regency Tamaya Resort and Spa, *BCS* s2.e1, "Switch" (2016). Courtesy of Sony Pictures Television.

the hotel bar later that night, Jimmy flips Kim from disapproving voice of reason to coconspirator in a raucous night of scamming. His wicked charisma is undeniable. You won't find this bar at the Tamaya; the scene was shot at Vintage 423, which is about half an hour away via I-25.

Santa Ana Pueblo is a world away from the concrete sprawl of Albuquerque, both visually and legally, but only takes about fifteen mins to drive there from the Duke City. The journey is a short drive north on the I-25; the pueblo is less than two miles from freeway exit 242. Although you'll be visiting a Hyatt hotel, entering the Tamaya Resort means you're entering federal land held in trust for Santa Ana Pueblo members as beneficiaries. The hotel's location makes a feature of the natural beauty around it. From the grounds on the property, you can enjoy stunning views of the cottonwoods by the Rio Grande, the Sandia Mountains, and the sacred Tuyuna Mesa. The Tamaya's Twin Warriors Golf Club is considered first class by many out-of-towners and locals alike.

In addition to the Oxbow Pool featured on *Better Call Saul*, the Tamaya has another two pools: the Plaza and Kiva. If you're visiting during the warmer parts of the year, you may wish to take a dunk. Access to a dip is only available for the hotel's overnight guests. The Plaza Grill offers waterside food at the Plaza Pool and you can take a beverage with you to the Oxbow Pool. If you go for dinner or a cocktail at the resort's main dining spot, the Rio Grande Lounge, you can view the Oxbow Pool from the restaurant's exterior. The contemporary Santa Ana Cafe has an Indigenous-influenced menu that provides local classics as well as vegetarian and gluten-free options, along with views of the Plaza Pool. It also has a to-go menu. The Trading Post general store also offers premade sandwiches, salads, snacks and coffee. The Atush Bar & Grille looks out on to the Twin Warriors Golf Course and offers breakfast lunch and cocktails. As a reminder, the only restaurant that provides a view of the Oxbow Pool is the Rio Grande Lounge. As a paying guest, you can bring seasonal snacks and beverages from the Plaza Grill with you to the Oxbow Pool.[1] If you're in luck, they might just have nachos.

Better Call Saul isn't the only famous show to have filmed at the resort. Season 17 of the reality show *The Bachelorette* was also filmed at the Tamaya in June 2021. Due to the COVID-19 pandemic, the resort was able to be used as a "bio-secure bubble" for the cast and crew.[2]

If you're an overnight guest, you can order poolside snacks in homage to Jimmy. Stop for lunch at the Santa Ana Cafe and enjoy a Vegan Rice Tofu Bowl, packed with southwestern flavors from the roast corn, zucchini, black beans, and cherry tomatoes.

COPPER CANYON CAFE $

a.k.a. Birdie's Homestyle Buffet, Amarillo
5455 Gibson Blvd. SE, Albuquerque, 87108
(505) 266-6318
coppercanyoncafeabq.com
Sunday–Saturday, 7:00 a.m.–3:00 p.m.

BCS s2.e3, "Amarillo," February 29, 2016

In the world of *Better Call Saul,* Birdie's Homestyle Buffet is in Amarillo, Texas. In the episode "Amarillo," Jimmy technically complies with the "no solicitation for business" rule to which lawyers are bound when they take the bar,[3] but doesn't stop him from engineering a series of events that deliver a literal busload of clients for the Sandpiper Crossing case. The scheme involves a lot of elders and a broken-down bus that drops them off at Birdie's to wait for "repairs" to their transportation.

This episode begins a rare on-screen love affair with old people, and it's fascinating to see how "elder law" is woven into Jimmy's story. As a cheesy opportunist, Jimmy is portrayed manipulating a vulnerable, somewhat gullible class of people, but because *Better Call*

FIGURE 55. Copper Canyon Café exterior, as Birdie's Homestyle Buffet, *BCS* s2.e3, "Amarillo" (2016). Courtesy of Sony Pictures Television.

Saul is a major TV show, the elder law plot twist puts a huge number of older faces on-screen, which isn't something you see very often. For example, *Better Call Saul* season 3, episode 9, "Fall," featuring Irene Landry (Jean Effron), also gives us a chance to get to know her spunky friends Rose (Carol Mansell), Myrtle (Phyllis Applegate), and Helen (Bonnie Bartlett).

But back to the eatery in question. The show used Copper Canyon Cafe's exterior for the Birdie's set. The café's existing exterior logo was covered with a blue sign advertising Birdie's. We see the broken-down bus parked outside the café, but we don't get a detailed shot of the interior or the food. In real life, Copper Canyon Cafe has a welcoming vibe and an interior filled with natural light. It serves homestyle classics with New Mexican and Mexican inspiration and, like Birdie's, the clientele is generally silver haired. Unlike Birdie's, it does not have a buffet. The all-day breakfast provides a range of savory and sweet options, and they have a generous list of customizable omelets. For lunch, try the Steakalada or the generous homemade soup and salad combo. If you're there on a cold day, there's nothing wrong with adding hot chocolate with whipped cream to your order.

Some readers may be unfamiliar with the type of food and eating experience Birdie's signifies. What is "homestyle" restaurant food anyway? What's homestyle for me probably differs from your definition of homestyle. For much of the twentieth century, the phrase was shorthand for unpretentious, affordable comfort food, but it is now somewhat unfashionable. Customers today seem more drawn to the sourcing of ingredients rather than the style of cooking. Today's restaurant buzzwords include *farm fresh*, *single origin*, or *in season*. By contrast, "homestyle" cooking is almost without seasons and significantly humbler in its food sourcing. *Merriam-Webster's Collegiate Dictionary* defines it as "having qualities (such as simplicity, familiarity, and lacking in pretention) associated with or evocative of home and especially home-cooked food," and dates the phrase back to 1869.[4]

Buffets have a somewhat grander provenance. The word *buffet* was around in sixteenth-century France, and the concept developed into a light supper served on a sideboard late at night, for example at nineteenth-century balls.[5] As with homestyle, it's a way of serving food that is not often replicated in contemporary eateries. Buffets are no longer considered opulent displays of wealth but are rather understood to be much more efficient and economical—think the American chain Golden Corral.

Order a Steakalada for a hearty lunch. If you're just dropping by, try out the indulgent hot chocolate.

EL MORENO RESTAURANTE Y PALETERIA $

a.k.a. El Michoacáno
2511 Isleta Blvd. SW, Albuquerque, 87105
(505) 244-8404
orderelmorenorestauranteypaleteria.com
Monday, Wednesday–Friday, 8:00 a.m.–5:00 p.m.
Saturday–Sunday, 7:00 a.m.–5:00 p.m.

BCS s2.e4, "Gloves Off," March 7, 2016
BCS s3.e6, "Off Brand," May 15, 2017
BCS s3.e8, "Slip," June 5, 2017
BCS s4.e8, "Coushatta," September 24, 2018
BCS s5.e1, "Magic Man," February 23, 2020
BCS s5.e2, "50% Off," February 24, 2020

We're about to have some fun with on-screen restaurant names and offscreen restaurants located in Albuquerque, so buckle up. The restaurant located on Isleta Boulevard is called El Moreno Restaurante y Paleteria. Its on-screen name in *Better Call Saul* is El Micho-

FIGURE 56. Tuco and Nacho take their cut of earnings from Krazy-8 (Maximino Arciniega) at El Michoacáno (El Moreno Restaurante y Paleteria), *BCS* s2.e4, "Gloves Off" (2016). Courtesy of Sony Pictures Television.

FIGURE 57. El Moreno exterior, 2022. Courtesy of Aimee Macpherson.

FIGURE 58. El Moreno chilaquiles, 2022. Courtesy of Aimee Macpherson.

acáno, the restaurant from which the Salamanca family manages its drug business. If you look up El Michoacáno in Albuquerque, you'll find a barrio taco food truck on the corner of San Pedro and Central that is unrelated to *Better Call Saul* but does make great tacos. Still with me? Moreover, La Michoacana de Paquime is the real-world name for El Griego Guiñador, a fictional Mexican-style restaurant that specializes in ice cream and serves as a front for the Salamanca clan to smuggle drugs across the US-Mexico border. To recap, while the on-screen names are El Michoacáno and El Griego Guiñador, the real-life restaurants are El Moreno Restaurante y Paleteria and La Michoacana de Paquime, respectively.

Let's move on to the restaurant itself. El Moreno's striking yellow exterior remains in place, along with the hand-painted red lettering outside, which ties in nicely with *Breaking Bad* and *Better Call Saul*'s use of red as a signal for criminal activity. Note the exterior sign on the restaurant was changed out for *Better Call Saul*; however, they used the restaurant's lighting box, so it's the same size and a similar color scheme. The interior mural on the long wall to the left as you enter is also part of the restaurant. In it, a young woman is sitting down, resting against a rock with her legs stretched out under a green skirt. She is looking up at a man whose face is concealed by a sombrero. He looks down at her while playing a guitar. At her feet is an empty water vessel. Behind her is what looks like an agave plant, and in the distance appear a small, flat-topped building and some trees. It's this mural that frames Tuco in "Gloves Off." When I visited, the two mariachi sombreros featured on-screen to the left of the cashier counter were in evidence hanging above the mural on either side. The terracotta roof over the cashier stand is still in place. However, the bar counter in the show is really an ice-cream counter that serves *paletas* and other frozen sweet treats.

I asked the cashier for a popular breakfast dish, and she recommended the chilaquiles. I went with over-easy eggs. I had salsa and homemade chips as an appetizer. The salsa was deep red and hot, like proper actual heat, and the corn chips were warm and golden. The chilaquiles arrived swiftly after the chips, and they did not disappoint. The egg yolks were notably golden and the crisp tortilla chips had only just been covered by shredded cheese and warmed tomato salsa. I also ordered a Jarritos Toronja (grapefruit soda). The server popped open the glass bottle in front of me at the table and poured it into a glass. I felt like I'd just ordered fine wine. It was zesty, bubbly, and semisweet.

Some subtle changes to note: The chairs are different on-screen. In the restaurant, they are a heavy wood, and in the show, they are padded leatherette with thin metal legs. These slimmer chairs let us view more of the actor in the shot than the blocky wooden chairs would. The brass espresso machine used by Nacho to make Hector's coffee in "Slip" was also brought in as a prop by the show. Nacho's introduction to Lalo in the back kitchen in "Coushatta" reminds viewers that the Salamancas take pleasure in cooking as well as killing. This kitchen is also a little different from its on-screen persona. In real life, it is larger and situated directly behind the cash register. It is not available for the public to view. The cooking done by Nacho's father, Manuel Varga (Juan Carlos Cantu), and Lalo was assisted by special effects to give the look of smoke and heat for the camera. The on-screen kitchen was dressed by the set decorating team for period-appropriate cookware.

The fare at El Moreno is made-from-scratch Mexican food served in the simple dining room you know from *Better Call Saul*. Although we see plenty of El Michoacáno at night on *Better Call Saul*, the real restaurant closes long before dark.

Try the *calda de res* for lunch. This is a beef broth packed with veggies like squash, corn, carrots, cabbage, and potatoes. It comes in two sizes, "chico" or "grande," with a side of rice, plus corn or flour tortillas. If you want to pay homage to Lalo Salamanca, get the asada tacos. Order a Jarrito soda with your meal and save some room to sample one of the paletas for dessert.

CARRIE'S RESTAURANT $$

Formerly Forque Kitchen and Bar
330 Tijeras Ave. NW, Albuquerque, 87102
(505) 302-6929
clydehotel.com/eat_drink/carrie_s_restaurant
Breakfast: Sunday–Saturday, 7:00 a.m.–10:30am
Lunch: Sunday–Saturday, 11:30 a.m.–1:30 p.m.

BCS s2.e6, "Bali Ha'i," March 21, 2016
BCS s3.e8, "Slip," June 5, 2017
BCS s4.e6, "Piñata," September 10, 2018
BCS s5.e4, "Namaste," March 9, 2010
BCS s5.e6, "Wexler v. Goodman," March 23, 2020
BCS s6.e3, "Rock and Hard Place," April 25, 2022

Forque Kitchen and Bar, "the quintessential location for both business and leisure travelers,"[6] is no more. Forque itself has been renamed Carrie's, after Clyde Tingley's wife, Carrie Wooster Tingley.

FIGURE 59. Kim, Kevin, and Paige cheers with their Moscow Mules at Forque (now Carrie's Restaurant). Kevin Wachtell (Rex Maynard Linn) is the CEO of Mesa Verde Bank and Trust, and Paige Novick (Cara Pifko) is the company's senior council. Kim bags the bank as a client for HHM early on in the show—and but for Chuck's intervention she would have easily secured them as her own client after leaving the firm. *BCS* s3.e8, "Slip" (2017). Courtesy of Sony Pictures Television.

FIGURE 60. Carrie's interior, 2022. Courtesy of Aimee Macpherson.

FIGURE 61. Carrie's Mule, 2022. Courtesy of Aimee Macpherson.

The Hyatt Regency, the building in which Forque was located, is now the Clyde Hotel, after Clyde Tingley, a former governor of New Mexico.[7] The building has undergone a renovation. Carrie's bar is a different business from former restaurant Forque, heavily featured on *Better Call Saul*. That said, there are some design details that show fans will recognize. The sunken dining space, square-backed dining chairs, and clouded glass droplights are all still in evidence. Today the lower part of the columns in the dining area are painted minty green. When I visited, there were several staff members who had started during the Forque days and remembered when the *Better Call Saul* crew would take over the restaurant. Grips would set up enormous black privacy screens around the set, keeping the action a secret.

The Moscow Mule cocktail ordered in almost every *Better Call Saul* scene is shot at this location. We're introduced to this iconic beverage in season 2's "Bali Ha'i"—the drink is associated with Kim Wexler, but it is Richard Schweikart (Dennis Boutsikaris) who orders it first. Kim rebuffs his invitation to day-drink and sticks with an ice tea, calling his choice "very vintage." Richard describes the drink as the best Moscow Mule in the city, and outlines the components of its success. After this encounter, Kim makes it her drink of choice at Forque.

Carrie's bar does have a variation of this drink on their bar menu, called Carrie's Mule. It's made with Expedition Vodka (from New Mexico distillery Santa Fe Spirits), lime, prickly pear juice, and ginger beer. The bartender working when I visited kindly accommodated me with a virgin Carrie's Mule. It's served in a burnished copper mug with a wedge of lime and a black straw. The mug I drank from at Carrie's had more of a patina than the brassy bright mug that Kim drinks from. The beverage itself is deep pink from the prickly pear juice, which gives the cocktail a southwestern spin. The opuntia plant (commonly referred to as prickly pear) can be found all over the state of New Mexico and populates the foothills of the Sandia Mountains as well as many Albuquerque front yards. There is even an annual Prickly Pear Festival in Albuquerque.[8]

Historically, the mule is something of a low-rent cocktail. It lacks the zest of a margarita or the sophistication of a French 75. Critics of the show have reflected on how such a faux classy cocktail matches Kim's tenuous and self-conscious grip on an establishment lifestyle.[9] Whether you buy into these projections or not, the copper mug certainly pops in the muted interior. So let's get a figurative round for Kim and wish her luck.

Forque was located on the ground floor of the Hyatt Regency hotel in Albuquerque's downtown. The show used much of the real restaurant on-screen, including the furniture and cutlery. For copyright reasons, the show switched out the art on the walls. These prints are only featured in the deep background, and yet this is the kind of attention to detail that drives home the care that goes into crafting *Better Call Saul*'s world, a subtly warped version of our own. Forque's anodyne luxury was the perfect fit for Kim's professional lunches: contemporary business casual to the marrow.

Much like the veneer of sophistication and establishment norms that Kim and Jimmy commit to at Forque, the restaurant itself had a more saucy history than the furnishings or "trendy and modern" menu would have you believe. Forque replaced a restaurant called McGrath's in 2011, which had occupied the restaurant space since 1990.[10] The namesake of this eatery was Lizzie McGrath, perhaps Albuquerque's most famous madame, and allegedly the city's richest woman. It took her name because the restaurant is located in what was once the city's red-light district (a.k.a. Hell's Half Acre).

As part of the Hyatt's rebranding in 2011, a mock funeral was organized in the New Orleans style to take down the McGrath's restaurant sign. The event even featured a hearse pulled by horses. The sign was lowered into a casket to the sound of bagpipes, while restaurant staff dressed in 1920s costume looked on.[11] The idea behind the spectacle was to ensure the restaurant's namesake, Lizzie, didn't haunt the new restaurant.

Order a Carrie's Mule for a pink southwestern twist on the classic.

LA MICHOACANA DE PAQUIME $

a.k.a. El Griego Guiñador
6500 Zuni Rd. SE, Albuquerque, 87108
(505) 266-3408
facebook.com/lamichoacanadepaquimeabq/?locale=es_LA
Sunday–Saturday, 11:00 a.m.–9:00 p.m.

BCS s2.e6, "Bali Ha'i," March 21, 2016
BCS s2.e8, "Fifi," April 4, 2016
BCS s3.e3, "Sunk Costs," April 24, 2017
BCS s3.e4, "Sabrosito," May 1, 2017

Paletas are a frozen treat made with cream (commonly from goat's or cow's milk) or water combined with signature flavors (for example, pieces of strawberry or tamarind paste) before they are frozen on a stick. At La Michoacana de Paquime, they've helpfully separated the options into "paletas de frutas" and "paletas de crema." You can also go for an agua fresca—and don't forget the option of adding spice to your paleta. If you're not into frozen treats, they have Frito pie, chips and salsa, and other savory snacks to

FIGURE 62. La Michoacana de Paquime interior, 2022. Courtesy of Aimee Macpherson.

FIGURE 63. La Michoacana de Paquime *paleta de fresa*, 2022. Courtesy of Aimee Macpherson.

try. The offerings are affordably priced and utterly delicious, so I encourage you to go all out. I personally love the coconut and raspberry paletas. But they also have more contemporary flavors like chicle (bubble gum), which comes in a brilliant aqua blue, and Oreo cookie.

You'll be pleased to know that the colorful murals inside and outside this paletería are part of the business. That means set dressing didn't paint over the palm trees or giant frozen chocolate bananas after the shoot. You can enjoy the business in much the same way it was shown in the show. Remember, please don't take a photo without purchasing something from the store—these folks have a business to run! Of course, there is one crucial difference from the version shown on-screen, and that's the name. In *Better Call Saul*, this paletería is called El Griego Guiñador, which the show subtitles translates as "the Winking Greek."

I don't think it's too outlandish to suggest that El Griego Guiñador is to the Salamancas what Los Pollos Hermanos is to Gus Fring, just on a significantly smaller scale (but don't tell them I said that). The Salamancas even use a fleet of frozen-goods trucks, named Regalo Helado, to transport their "ice cream" (wink, wink) from Mexico to North America. The name La Michoacana probably sounds familiar to fans of *Better Call Saul*, because it's close to the name of the Salamancas' other Albuquerque café, El Michoacáno.

We first encounter El Griego in season 2's "Bali Ha'ai." Unfortunately, neither Hector nor Mike enjoy the ice cream, although there is certainly an ice-cold tenor to their exchange. Hector does have his signature espresso in a cup and saucer—an elegant touch but unavailable at the location in real life. By the time season 3 features the paletería, both it and the Regalo Helado truck are something of a breadcrumb trail for those out to complicate life for the Salamancas. In season 3, episode 4, "Sabrosito," we enjoy yet another nighttime stakeout by Mike outside; the DEA raids this shop at night in act 1.

The Regalo Helado truck gets a dramatic introduction at the opening of "Fifi" in season 2. The lengthy single-crane shot creates a masterful portrayal of our ice-cream truck's frequent, stressful journey through the border crossing. Film buffs are sure keen to point out a likeness to the *Touch of Evil* opening crane shot, which also portrays the border between Mexico and North America.

It only seems reasonable that the driver, Ximenez Lecerda (Manuel Uriza), takes out a popsicle to refresh himself after the truck passes inspection. This is the first time we see one of El Griego's frozen treats: they are introduced to us as part of a criminal activity, long before we see the paletería where they are sold. This removes the popsicle's status as an innocent sweet treat. Much like fried chicken, pepperoni pizza, or mint chocolate chip ice cream, we can't see the food in the *Breaking Bad / Better Call Saul* universe without also seeing the criminal underworld it signifies.

The origin of the name La Michoacana? Well, it's complicated. The name translates into English as "from the state of Michoacán" in Mexico, a bit like the noun "Texan" referring to someone who is from Texas. The name is used in many ways as a proprietary eponym in Mexico, much like "Kleenex" or "Google." However the question of whether "La Michoacana" has been truly genericized is still up for debate. I'll refer you to a long article on Eater regarding the history and trademark legal battles surrounding "La Michoacana" and who may use the name in North America.[12] The sweet treat itself dates back to the 1930s in Tocumbo, Mexico. For a deeper dive into the Albuquerque paleta scene, look up Candolin Cook's article "The Big Chill," which outlines an excellent selection of frozen treats in the 505.[13]

Sidenote: Make sure you're headed to La Michoacana de Paquime on Zuni. There is another La Michoacana de Paquime at 6501 Central Avenue NW and several more paleterías with similar names throughout the city, including La Michoacana del Centro, La Michoacana del Sur 2, and La Estrella Michoacana.

Enjoy at least one paleta from this landmark store. Explore the menu and try a flavor that's new to you.

NOTES

1. Hyatt Regency Tamaya Resort and Spa, "Dining," accessed February 26, 2024, https://www.hyatt.com/hyatt-regency/en-US/tamay-hyatt-regency-tamaya-resort-and-spa/dining.
2. Wikipedia, s.v. "*The Bachelorette* (American season 17)," last modified December 9, 2023, 10:04, https://en.wikipedia.org/wiki/The_Bachelorette_(American_season_17).
3. American Bar Association, *Model Rules of Professional Conduct*, "Rule 7.3 Solicitation of Clients," April 17, 2019, https://www.americanbar.org/groups/professional_responsibility/publications/model_rules_of_professional_conduct/rule_7_3_direct_contact_with_prospective_clients/.
4. *Merriam-Webster*, s.v. "homestyle (*adj.*)," accessed March 16, 2022, https://www.merriam-webster.com/dictionary/homestyle#h1.
5. Wikipedia, s.v. "Buffet," last modified December 7, 2023, 11:46, https://en.wikipedia.org/wiki/Buffet.
6. Clyde Hotel, "Carrie's Restaurant," accessed February 5, 2024, https://www.clydehotel.com/eat_drink/carrie_s_restaurant/.
7. Matthew Narvaiz, "Hyatt Regency Downtown to Rebrand as the Clyde Hotel," *Albuquerque Journal*, March 21, 2022.
8. New Mexico Prickly Pear Festival, home page, accessed July 3, 2022, https://nmpricklypearfest.com/.
9. Leigh Kunkel, "To Understand 'Better Call Saul's' Kim Wexler, Look at Her Drink Order," *Eater*, June 29, 2017, https://www.eater.com/2017/6/29/15861960/better-call-saul-kim-wexler-moscow-mule.
10. Rivkela Brodsky, "McGrath's Grill Laid to Rest after 20 Years," *Albuquerque Journal*, May 16, 2011.

11. Brodsky, "McGrath's Grill Laid to Rest."

12. Serena Maria Daniels, "The Paleta War," *Eater*, October 22, 2019, https://www.eater.com/2019/10/22/20908347/la-michoacana-paleta-legal-battle.

13. Candolin Cook, "The Big Chill," *The Bite*, accessed May 16, 2023, https://thebitenm.com/the-big-chill-an-albuquerque-paleta-round-up/.

LEVEL 5 $$

2000 Bellamah Ave. NW, Albuquerque, 87104
(505) 318-3998
hotelchaco.com/eat_drink/level-5
Brunch: Saturday–Sunday, 8:00 a.m.–1:00 p.m.
Dinner: Sunday–Saturday, 4:00 p.m.–10:00 p.m.

BCS s4.e2, "Breathe," August 13, 2018

Level 5 at Hotel Chaco has only appeared in the show's universe once, and that was in "Breathe." But it's a location that packs a punch for fans of Lydia Rodarte-Quayle. The iconic shot is of Lydia on the phone with Gus from one of the sofas on the restaurant's roof-deck. When you exit the elevator on level 5, walk through the bar. Lydia's accent chair was to the right of the patio. The chair was part of the level 5 decor scheme, and at the time of writing, the same style is still in use on the patio. In the scene, a stone ottoman to her left holds a white cup and saucer with a little spoon, but we don't see her drink from it.

Odds are you aren't visiting this restaurant to make a call to one

FIGURE 64. Lydia at Hotel Chaco's Level 5 rooftop restaurant, *BCS* s4.e2, "Breathe" (2018). Courtesy of Sony Pictures Television.

of TV's most infamous villains, so I suggest you don't visit the place in the blinding midday sun and instead choose to go at sunset and take in the beautiful view and enjoy a fresh juice or cocktail from the bar.

This location is something of a *Breaking Bad* reunion for cast and crew. Not only do we see two crossover characters from *Breaking Bad* (Lydia and Mike, three if you count Gus on the phone), but the episode was written by Thomas Schnauz and directed by Michelle MacLaren, both of whom worked extensively on *Breaking Bad*. In fact, they both worked with Vince Gilligan before *Breaking Bad*, on *The X-Files* season 9. MacLaren was coproducer on *The X-Files* but made her debut as a director with season 9, episode 7, "John Doe," written by Vince Gilligan. Schnauz penned *X-Files* season 9, episode 5, "Lord of the Files."

Hotel Chaco is a relatively new build (it opened in 2017) that is owned by Heritage Hotels & Resorts. On its website, Chaco is described as a "AAA 4 diamond boutique hotel."[1] The menu at Level 5 was put together by chef Marc Quiñones, who graduated on the President's Lists of the Scottsdale Culinary Institute. You can visit Level 5 for brunch, dinner, or a cocktail. A standout item on the menu is Chef Marc's New Mexico Spiced Duck Fat Fried Oysters, which won third place at the 2017 and 2018 Great American Seafood Cook-Off in New Orleans. The dish comes with warm chorizo salad, Chimayó blackened toast, and preserved lemon. The menu features many contemporary twists on traditional New Mexican food, such as tostadas made with foie gras and *calabacitas* served with asparagus and red chile fluid gel. Situated on the top of a relatively tall building (for Albuquerque), Level 5 towers above much of the city and showcases excellent views of the Sandia Mountains.

While you're taking in the view from Level 5, walk to the farthest right of the roof-deck and you should be able to see the roof of Hotel Albuquerque (it's literally adjacent to Hotel Chaco). Hotel Albuquerque was where the legendary *Breaking Bad* season finale party took place for cast and crew. Technically called a "wrap party" at the end of each season, it's a small but sincere way for the production to give thanks to all the blood, sweat, and 3 a.m. wake-ups for the people who are in the business of executing a TV episode. It's perhaps fitting then that *Better Call Saul* had a wrap party for season 4 at Level 5 itself, overlooking the final partying spot of its prequel. So when you're up there, raise a glass to the crew whose hard work went into making the shows such fun to watch.

Make your way up to Level 5 to take in the view on a comfortable lounge chair while sipping a lavender chamomile craft tea from the New Mexico Tea Company. If you'd like to soy milk, the menu offers it as an add-on in the "Craft Coffee" section.

FANTASY WORLD

$$$

5000 Jefferson St. NE, Albuquerque, 87109
(505) 433-4239
fantasyworld-nm.com/location
Sunday–Saturday, 9:00 p.m.–5:00 a.m.

BCS s4.e8, "Coushatta," September 24, 2018

In this episode, German engineers are delivered, in a windowless van, to Fantasy World for some entertainment. It's an attempt to provide them with a break from the pressures of their secret construction work on Gus Fring's superlab in the hope they will get back to work with greater zeal. Their leader, Werner Ziegler (Rainer Bock), is unable to relax at the bar, and Mike decides to relocate him to the more subdued Louie's Pub and Grill. Werner's team members, however, have no problem letting off a lot of steam enjoying the performers. Kai (Ben Bela Böhm) starts to rabble-rouse, which gets him kicked out, but not before we see some dancers at work. Most of the local talent you seen dancing on the screen were sourced locally by the Extras Casting department. Although strippers are on-screen, this scene and the scene from 4's Cabaret in *Breaking Bad* season 3 do not focus on erotica. Instead, these venues are forums for taking a closer

FIGURE 65. Fantasy World rear exterior, 2022. Courtesy of Aimee Macpherson.

FIGURE 66. Fantasy World front exterior, 2022. Courtesy of Aimee Macpherson.

look at the emotional state of our characters. We notice them feel uncomfortable (Werner, Mike) or overexcited (Jesse, at 4's Cabaret). The almost desexualized atmosphere portrayed at these strip clubs reminds me of Roland Barthes's comments on the French striptease, where he describes how the Moulin Rouge seems "less to abolish eroticism than to domesticate it."[2] Erotica in this episode is stress-relief service for some captive engineers. Jesse blowing Walt's life savings at a strip club may seem like a weakness, but the money was for buying an RV to convert into a meth cooking lab. Cooking meth is an illegal activity that makes visiting a perfectly legal strip club seem comparatively wholesome, even if you're spending someone else's money. In this way, the stripteases of *Breaking Bad* and *Better Call Saul* are almost given a "reassuringly petite bourgeois status."[3]

Fantasy World kindly granted the show permission to use its real name. Unlike the club's on-screen bar, you cannot order liquor at Fantasy World; New Mexico regulations dictate that only nonalcoholic beverages can be served at nude bars. The real-deal Fantasy World beverage bar provides, instead, a lot of caffeinated drinks. If you're looking for a Monster Energy at 4:00 a.m. on a Wednesday, this is the place. There is a store on the property called the Mall, where you can purchase toys, clothes, and games (all in the theme of sex and erotica, of course). The setup is a traditional one—performers are female, and the audience is generally all male. And as a reminder, patrons are required to be eighteen years of age or older. Today the exterior is a dark gray-black, but it still has the maroon awnings featured on the show. The entrance is in the back, and that is the entrance used for the on-screen drama. Fantasy World sits on the same lot as a custard-yellow building called HappyDaze Cannabis. It's right by the on-ramp for the Pan American Freeway NE, opposite a large gas station.

PRODUCTION PRACTICALITIES

Standards and Practices, or "S&P," as it's known to the crew, is the department tasked with making sure content adheres to the TV network's guidelines, including those regarding the portrayal of sex, violence, and profanities. This is self-regulation of a kind, and it means the network can force the show to remove, edit, or reshoot content that they disagree with on the grounds of S&P—and it creates a lot of work when shooting scenes in a strip club. To save everyone time and money, much discussion and care go into the question of what is going to be on-camera. Shot lists of this nature are usually negotiated and finalized between the production and the S&P department before the camera rolls so that everyone is on the same page about what will and will not (for example, nipples and bottoms) be featured. A shooting script may just read "Early evening, strip club. Davie walks to the bar," but the shot list will have more detail about who the director is planning to have in the shot. That involves how much the camera will capture of what they are doing and how much they are wearing.

Order a Red Bull and enjoy the show!

PENNY'S DINER

$

a.k.a. diner open late
2101 Camino Del Llano, Belen, 87002
(505) 861-3181
facebook.com/pennysdinerbelen
Sunday–Saturday, open 24 hours

BCS s4.e9, "Wiedersehen," October 1, 2018

Penny's of Belen is part of a franchise of Penny's Diners. There are almost thirty of these restaurants across the United States. The Penny's in Belen has a shiny metal exterior that evokes railroad dining cars on trains in the 1950s and earlier. The franchise, founded in 1994, was named Penny after the wife of the president

FIGURE 67 Exterior of Penny's Diner in Belen, 2022. Courtesy of Aimee Macpherson.

FIGURE 68. Penny's hand-dipped strawberry malt, 2022. Courtesy of Aimee Macpherson.

of Avantic Lodging Enterprises.[4] The restaurant's compact booths and chrome finishes bring the exterior look inside, making it hard to forget the diner's railroad origins. Route 66 memorabilia adorns the walls, and the floor is black-and-white checkered tile. Penny's is open twenty-four hours a day and serves breakfast all the time. The menu also offers historic American sweet treats like pie á la mode and hand-dipped milkshakes and malts. This means that their shakes and malts are made by scooping ice cream and milk, or ice cream and malt powder, into a blender by hand—rather than pumping them out of a preprepared shake machine like you would with a McFlurry. Pie with ice cream and malts are part of American food history, and their growth in popularity goes hand in hand with the history of mechanized food processing. Malt-based supplements were developed for infants by James Horlick in the 1800s.[5] The name "malted milk" was trademarked in 1887,[6] which gives you a sense of just how long people have been drinking it. Soon people were just ordering it for the taste. *Pie á la mode* means "fashionable pie" and has been served in North America since the 1880s. John Gieriet of the Hotel la Perl is credited with inventing it.[7] When you order these desserts (which you really should!), you are ordering dishes that have been on the menu in North America for over a hundred years.

Penny's Diner is located in Belen, thirty-five miles south of Albuquerque via I-25 South. *Belen* is the Spanish word for Bethlehem, where Jesus was born. There are cities named Belen across the world in Turkey, Argentina, and Bolivia, to name but a few. Belen, New Mexico, was founded in 1740 and called Nuestra Señora de Belén (Our Lady of Bethlehem).[8] It has a complicated and war-torn history. As for food history, allegedly, Belen is the original home of the waffle fry. In 1950, William F. Beavers, owner of B&B Cafe on Becker Avenue, filed the first patent for a machine that "sliced potatoes into waffle-like slices."[9] It's hard to corroborate the legend, so take it with a pinch of salt. B&B Cafe is no longer in operation but the menu at Penny's does offer waffle fries.

One of the restaurant's staff members told me on a Friday night that this Penny's can get busy with the locals under twenty-one, who sit at the bar top and order lavish shakes and malts. In cinema, the innocent and childlike nature of diner food and drink is frequently contrasted with the sinister dealings of those who are criminal or simply on the run. On-screen baddies have been slurping milkshakes or starting shootouts in diners for many years. From hard-boiled dramas in the 1940s to their nostalgic copycats in the 1990s, here are some of the most famous: *Fallen Angel* (1945), *The Killers* (1946), *Taxi Driver* (1976), *Sudden Impact* (1983), *Natural Born Killers* (1994), *Pulp Fiction* (1994), *Mulholland Drive* (2001), and *Looper* (2012). So when Jimmy and Kim choose a diner to celebrate pulling off an illegal scheme, they are just another entry in the catalog of cinematic characters who are most certainly up to no good.

The crackling neon of the diner's exterior is really allowed to show off in the establishing shot of the restaurant featured in the episode "Wiedersehen," German for "until we meet again" or "goodbye for the present." Inside, the low overhead lighting casts a shine on the booth's melamine benches. As Kim and Jimmy beam at each other in the cramped booth, the glassy window behind them creates a glow on their skin, echoed in the diner's shiny chrome fixtures and benches. They seem rejuvenated, energized, jubilant about the success of their scam, their codependency further deepened by this latest criminal activity. Jimmy is drinking a cup of hot coffee, while Kim doesn't eat or drink anything. It seems a strange way to celebrate—abstaining. But perhaps she has all she wants to eat right in front of her, in the form of Slippin' Jimmy. As he points out, Kim obviously has a growing appetite for crossing the line with him. The sex appeal of doing wrong is obviously not dampened by his unkinky outfit (T-shirt and wraparound shades dangling from sporty straps around his neck).

Order a strawberry malt for a nostalgic diner experience.

MONTE CARLO STEAKHOUSE AND LIQUOR STORE $$

a.k.a. karaoke bar
3916 Central Ave. SW, Albuquerque, 87105
(505) 836-9886
facebook.com/people/Monte-Carlo-Steakhouse-and-Liquor-Store/100063747482461/
Tuesday–Saturday, 11:00 a.m.–10:00 p.m.

BCS s4.e10, "Winner," October 8, 2018

In "Winner," we visit the Monte Carlo in a flashback to 1998. It's the location for a party celebrating Jimmy's new qualification as a lawyer. Jimmy gets up and starts singing "The Winner Takes It All" (1980) by ABBA, and then invites his big brother to join him for a duet. Karaoke is supposed to be feel-good, right? Swedish supergroup ABBA and karaoke go together like bread and butter. But in this moment, I get chills down my spine . . . who is the winner of these embittered siblings? In the flashback, Chuck's faux shyness is coaxed away by Jimmy, and when he seizes the microphone, we see a guy who loves to dominate. Actor Michael McKean's well-tuned

FIGURE 69. Chuck and Jimmy's karaoke duet at Monte Carlo Steakhouse, *BCS* s4.e10, "Winner" (2018). Courtesy of Sony Pictures Television.

singing cuts a jarring note over the distantly amateur-hour tone of the evening, which it fits with Chuck's unrelenting professionalism. He even sings like a pro! The man's ambition is tireless.

But who led the horse to water? Jimmy. And for every value Chuck represents, Jimmy drives in the opposite direction. Flash-forward and the ideological divorce between these two siblings, the cost of winning, couldn't be clearer. In case it wasn't obvious enough, we do get to circle back to this harrowing moment when Jimmy doles out career advice to a "marked" young woman. Kristy Esposito (Abby Quinn) has put herself forward for Chuck's legacy scholarship. She's a convicted shoplifter. For most of the lawyers on the nominating committee, her rap sheet automatically rules her out. For Jimmy, that crime is the exact reason she deserves to win. If she's changed her life—she shouldn't have to live in the shadow of a past mistake. The establishment's flat-out refusal to see the person she became after the conviction strikes a terrible chord for Jimmy, and we get a peek into Chuck's emotional brutality toward his younger brother. Much like a toddler who is branded "difficult," Jimmy tries to convince the partners that the label becomes self-fulfilling. And this scholarship is a shot to break that cycle. Of course, it's rejected, so Jimmy tries to impart to Kirsty some hard-won life advice: you're always going to be judged for that conviction, so the only way you're going to succeed is by owning it. "Remember—the *winner* takes it all." And we are reminded with a jolt of the moment between two brothers smiling at each as they perform their ominous duet.

The tonal blue of the flashback sequence makes the Monte Carlo venue kind of hard to make out. It also makes the bar feel cold and unwelcoming, a further reminder of the unsettling power struggle between the two brothers. In real life, the Monte Carlo Steakhouse is bathed in warm yellow light—courtesy of no windows except in the front, which faces Central Avenue—with comfortable deep-red leatherette banquettes and a welcoming vibe. When I visited, every table was full and there was a short wait to be seated (the restaurant doesn't take reservations). The decor feels like a personal collection of Americana: the wood-paneled walls are lined with framed portraits of old-time famous Americans like Elvis Presley and Marilyn

Monroe, and plastic flowers rest above the booths. It does have a fine collection of decorative drinking paraphernalia (including vintage glasses and neon), which ought not to be a surprise given that it's also home to a package liquor store. When I went inside, the cashier was conversing with his friend, both seated at a white table. White shelves filled with beer, wine, and liquor lined the walls, sectioned off with a small chain, which one of the store workers removed so I could take a look around.

The charbroiler in the corner of the restaurant enables you to see the flames on the grill from your table. Offerings are extensive, and the menu includes definitions of charbroiled terms, so you understand (and take responsibility for) what you're ordering—for example, medium rare (warm center), medium (pink center), and medium well (no pink). Plus, they offer traditional Greek food like souvlaki (smallish cubes of meat grilled over an open flame) as a main dish and baklava (chopped and toasted pistachio nuts layered between filo pastry and stuck together with honey) for dessert. Their burger is an impressive half pound of charbroiled ground sirloin with all the fixings and hand-cut fries.

The Monte Carlo has a loyal following, and the steaks are no-frills delicious. If you are looking for a meat-free route, they also offer salad, Texas toast, soup of the day, and baked potatoes, which come wrapped in tinfoil with a side of whipped butter and sour cream. Add to that mix all the delights of a full bar and you have a great evening on your hands. Given it's also a packaged liquor store, you can purchase alcohol to take home with you. The bar also serves non-alcoholic beverages, and there are free refills for soft drinks, coffee, tea, and milk, so no matter your preferences, there is no need to suffer with plain ol' iced water.

It's important to take note that this classic eatery does not offer karaoke like we see on-screen. Nor are there pearlized helium balloons; that would cramp their style. The steak house has been going since 1970, and still cuts its own steaks.[10] It was even featured on Guy Fieri's Food Network show *Diners, Drive-Ins, and Dives* in an episode called "Where the Locals Go" (2008). All I have to add is "and so should you!"

Go for a fourteen-ounce boneless New York strip charbroiled to your preference, with a baked potato on the side.

NOTES

1. Hotel Chaco, "Hotel Chaco," accessed March 28, 2022, https://www.hotelchaco.com/.

2. Roland Barthes, *Mythologies: The Complete Edition, in a New Translation*, trans. Richard Howard and Annette Lavers (New York: Hill and Wang, 2012), 167.

3. Barthes, *Mythologies*, 167–68.

4. Penny's Diner, "About," accessed February 5, 2024, https://www.pennysdiner.com/about/.

5. Wikipedia, s.v. "Malted milk," last modified January 26, 2024, 12:58, https://en.wikipedia.org/wiki/Malted_milk.

6. Wisconsin Historical Society, "That's Meat and Drink to Me: Wisconsin's Malted Milk Story," accessed March 16, 2022, https://www.wisconsinhistory.org/museum/exhibits/horlicks/.

7. Wikipedia, s.v. "Pie á la Mode," last modified December 12, 2023, 15:55, https://en.wikipedia.org/wiki/Pie_%C3%A0_la_Mode#cite_ref-8.

8. City of Belen, New Mexico (website), "About," accessed March 16, 2022, https://www.belen-nm.gov/about/.

9. Wikipedia, s.v. "Belen, New Mexico," last modified January 18, 2024, 12:49, https://en.wikipedia.org/wiki/Belen,_New_Mexico.

10. Gil Garduño, "Monte Carlo Steakhouse—Albuquerque, New Mexico," *Gil's Thrilling (and Filling) Blog*, August 24, 2023, https://www.nmgastronome.com/?p=344.

Grandma's K&I Diner $$

a.k.a. Missouri diner
2500 Broadway Blvd. SE, Albuquerque, 87102
(505) 243-1881
grandmaskandidiner.com
Sunday–Saturday, 7:00 a.m.–3:00 p.m.

BCS s5.e1, "Magic Man," February 23, 2020

In *Better Call Saul* season 4, episode 1, "Smoke," our favorite Cinnabon manager is spooked by his interaction with the nurse at the hospital and the following taxi ride with Jeff (still played by Don Harvey in this season), the Albuquerque cabbie. Fast-forward to season 5's "Magic Man," in which Gene decides to leave town for a few days. He switches out his Nebraska license plate for a Missouri one, which gives us a good idea of where he's headed. (Friendly reminder: Kansas City, Missouri, is Kim's hometown.) We meet Grandma's K&I Diner on an empty snowy road. On-screen, the exterior of the diner got a little help from postproduction, when they digitally removed

FIGURE 70. Grandma's K&I Diner exterior, 2022. Courtesy of Aimee Macpherson.

FIGURE 71. Grandma's K&I interior clock, 2022. Courtesy of Aimee Macpherson.

FIGURE 72. Grandma's K&I Travis burrito, 2022. Courtesy of Aimee Macpherson.

many of the neighboring buildings featured in the wide shots. This helped to place the diner in Kansas City rather than the real diner's location in Albuquerque's South Valley. This kind of special effects work is common on many television shows, but it's somewhat unusual on *Better Call Saul* and *Breaking Bad*. Where possible, the shows did as much work "in camera"—on set—rather than during the edit. The phone booth outside the diner is a show prop and won't be in evidence on your visit, but the name of the restaurant and most of its interior decor is the real deal.

Grandma's K&I Diner opened in 1960,[1] and it doesn't seem like the interior or exterior have changed much since. Exterior signage boasts "Home of the Travis." The what? The Travis is a burrito with beans and beef, smothered in red or green chile (or both), cheese, lettuce, and tomato, then smothered in french fries. I hear a full one weighs almost eight pounds. The menu outlines three sizes:

> As seen on *Man v. Food*
> **Full Travis**: For those with a huge appetite
> **Half Travis**: For those whose eyes are as big as their stomach
> **Wimp Travis**: Enjoy the famous Travis with no shame

I ordered the Wimp, plus a cup of coffee. Both were served on colorful Fiestaware plates. Unafraid of carbs, I was excited to try this new combo. The generous pile of fries meant my knife and fork did serious work searching for the burrito underneath. Soft flour tortilla and crisp french fries deliver a forkful that is both hearty and compelling. Marrying the flour tortilla and potato fries with sauce ensures the bite isn't dry. I chose green chile and found it fresh with a medium level of heat. The coffee came with plenty of refills, ensuring I stayed awake despite a belly full of Travis. There are photos on the walls of several customers who have done battle with this dish and won. I don't know who the Travis is named after, but I can attest it is a substantial legacy.

Of course, Gene does not tuck into a burrito of any shape or size at this diner because it would be a dead giveaway for New Mexico, and story-wise we're in Kansas. He orders but does not eat pancakes. This diner does offer pancakes, which start as a stack of two with syrup before you add optional sides like a bacon or egg.

Many show fans have remarked on the clock in this diner sequence. There is indeed a clock in this restaurant, located on the wall at the entryway to the kitchen. However, it's a different make, and in a different spot than the one we see on the show. This Easter egg takes a little explaining, so bear with me. Gene gives a hard stare to a prop clock that clearly shows the time, 12:16. Now, is anything a coincidence on this show? It's hard not to remember season 3, episode 5, "Chicanery," when Chuck exclaims, "I knew it was 12:16! One after the Magna Carta."[2] Chuck, humiliated by Jimmy on the stand, is referring to the Mesa Verde Bank and Trust files debacle. Jimmy switched up Chuck's documents so he would remember an incorrect address for the proposed new Mesa Verde branch. Chuck told the bank the incorrect address, 1216 Rosella Drive, Scottsdale, Arizona, which was planted by Jimmy. The correct address was 1261 Rosella Drive. Chuck being Chuck, he doubles down on his mistake, which sours his relationship with the bank, delays the hearing, and puts his mental clarity into question.

After his stint at the diner in "Magic Man," Gene returns to Nebraska. The previous five seasons of *Better Call Saul* open with

Gene at Cinnabon, but season 6 doesn't show us Gene until episode 10. By this point in Gene's timeline, he doesn't shy away from Jeff's knowledge that he is Saul Goodman. Over the next few episodes, Gene uses Saul's reputation to trick Jeff the cabbie (played by Pat Healy in season 6) and Jeff's friend Buddy (Max Bickelhaup) into thinking they will learn the rules of "the game" they so desperately want to join. While Gene does teach Jeff and Buddy scams that Jimmy McGill would be proud of, like how to rob a department store, then steal bank account information from drunk rich men, he stops there. But Gene goes on to manipulate, blackmail, and humiliate Jeff *and* his mom, Marion (played by the legendary Carol Burnett), with the audacity and skill set of Saul Goodman. The script for the series finale, "Saul Gone," shows us the exact moment Gene flips the switch and goes full Saul. Scene 25 kicks off with Gene locked in a small holding cell, furious at himself for getting caught because of Jeff and Buddy's incompetence. A piece of graffiti on the ceiling changes his perspective: "MY LAWYR WILL REEM U ASSHOLES." This statement finally unlocks his superpowers as a criminal lawyer—"he's SAUL FUCKING GOODMAN," the script notes read. And from that moment on, the script replaces Gene with Saul: "Saul (let's call him that, that's who he is!)."[3]

Go to Grandma's K&I to brood on Jimmy/Saul/Gene's many complex identities, but stay for a Travis. You just have to worry about which size to choose.

JUANITA'S COMIDA MEXICANA

$

a.k.a. Bienvenidos Amigos
910 Fourth St. SW, Albuquerque, 87102
(505) 843-9669
facebook.com/JuanitasComidaMexicana/?locale=es_LA
Monday–Saturday, 8:00 a.m.–3:30 p.m.

BCS s5.e2, "50% Off," February 24, 2020

The restaurant's show name, Bienvenidos Amigos, is painted on the real business's building below the main window. One big difference between reality and television is the bright-blue grill on the front of the restaurant. It was removed for the show, enabling the café window to serve as a frame for the inside action. At Bienvenidos Amigos, Nacho witnesses the intimidation of his father, Manuel, by the Salamanca clan, concealed from view outside. Much like L. B. Jeffrie's view of his neighbors in *Rear Window* (1953), Nacho's view of his father is tense yet passive. We can't hear the dialogue, so this moment creates tension between characters without relying on exposition. Although the scene is shot at night, this restaurant doesn't operate after dark.

FIGURE 73. Juanita's Comida Mexicana exterior, as Bienvenidos Amigos, *BCS* s5.e2, "50% Off" (2020). Courtesy of Sony Pictures Television.

FIGURE 74 Breakfast burrito at Juanita's Comida Mexicana, 2022. Courtesy of Aimee Macpherson.

Comida mexicana translates to "Mexican food," and this eatery is a great excuse to visit the Barelas neighborhood in Albuquerque. Barelas started out as a little village dating back to the seventeenth century. With the arrival of the railroads in the late nineteenth century, it was engulfed by the city of Albuquerque. In the 1920s, Fourth Street—the main road through Barelas—formed part of Route 66. With the closure of the railroads and redirection of the highways, this area went through several decades of economic distress. Recently, art galleries and coffee shops have opened in the neighborhood. Juanita's exterior looks like a repurposed pump station from the early twentieth century.

When I arrived at Juanita's midmorning, a white pickup truck full of hay sat in the restaurant parking lot. Unlike the open door in the show, there are two side-by-side push doors to get inside. It's a little crowded inside, in the best way. As I walked in, I was met with poinsettia flower oilcloths, the TV running a singing contest at low volume, and a wide variety of very healthy houseplants. I sat down at a table by the barred front window. On the windowsill, several plants nestled in *molcajete* bowls of various sizes, and below them was a hand-painted mural dedicated to the Sierra Tarahumara, located in the Mexican state of Chihuahua. I ordered a breakfast burrito with sausage and green chile. The eggs were done just like they're done at the Grove, in an omelet-style scramble that's popped inside the burrito before the whole thing is rolled up. I couldn't resist adding a small cup of horchata, no ice, in a red plastic cup. They also have Mexican Coca-Cola, which means it's made with real cane sugar, not the high-fructose corn syrup found in American Coca-Cola, and served in a glass bottle.

Juanita's has a special for every day they are open, but don't sleep on their regular lunch plates. If you haven't tried a flauta yet, now is the time. It is a large flour tortilla (the same size you'd use in making a burrito) curled into a thin cigar-like shape around a savory filling, usually chicken or shredded beef. The whole thing is then deep fried, resulting in a crunchy exterior and a soft filling. Sold in pairs, the flautas are substantial enough for a light snack or as a side to your main lunch plate.

Try a breakfast burrito or the flautas at this friendly eatery. Wash it down with a Mexican Coca-Cola.

THE 66 PIT STOP

$

a.k.a. Alejo Travel Center
14311 Central Ave. NW, Albuquerque, 87121
(505) 552-7762
thelagunaburger.com/menus-and-locations
Sunday–Saturday, 6:00 a.m.–7:00 p.m.

BCS s5.e9, "Bad Choice Road," April 13, 2020

New Mexicans, it will shock you to learn that Laguna Burger wasn't used as a restaurant in *Better Call Saul*. On-screen, this restaurant's name is replaced with the moniker Alejo Travel Center. Mike and Jimmy wait outside to be rescued by Gus's henchmen, Tyrus (Ray Campbell) and Victor, after their harrowing odyssey in the desert. Directly behind them is the stucco gray-and-white wall of the travel center, the same color as the restaurant wall today. On-screen right, to Jimmy's left, the concrete awning frames a series of red poles in the ground circling a drainage system. Behind that are whispers of scrappy brush; in the distance, piles of construction sand foreground a modestly

FIGURE 75. The 66 Pit Stop exterior, 2022. Courtesy of Aimee Macpherson.

FIGURE 76. Bikers rest at the 66 Pit Stop eating area, 2022. Courtesy of Aimee Macpherson.

FIGURE 77. 66 Pit Stop Laguna Burger, 2022. Courtesy of Aimee Macpherson.

sized mesa. The sky above is baby blue and almost cloudless. There is no shade, and the hard weather of this beautiful landscape leaves its mark on Jimmy's and Mike's sunburned faces and chapped lips.

The location evokes artist Edward Ruscha's *Standard Station* (1966). (I strongly urge you to seek out his book *Twentysix Gasoline Stations*, first published in 1963, featuring, you guessed it, twenty-six photographs of gas stations along Route 66 between Los Angeles and Oklahoma. Tate Modern's website has an excellent online free version of the book.[4]) Ruscha's work is responsible for the popularization of a Californian pop-art aesthetic fascinated with the commonplace, the everyday, and even the ugly aspects of contemporary life. It's commonly thought that his compilation of gas station photographs, in sequential order along Route 66, are emblematic of the stations of the cross.[5] These gas stations are markers of suffering on a journey toward death, and, eventually, rebirth. We can use this to get a bit lyrical with our description of Jimmy. He went out into the desert, endured intense suffering, and arguably laid the old Jimmy to rest. In limbo at the gas station, it is only a matter of time before he is brought back to town with Lalo's cash, reborn as Saul Goodman.

I arrived at the 66 Pit Stop the day after American outlaw biker, author, and actor Sonny Barger's death was announced in the news. I hadn't given a thought to my timing until I went to park my car and saw more than twenty Harley-Davidson motorcycles lined up neatly outside. Luggage, including a few small wheeled carry-on bags, were strapped or taped to the back of most of the bikes. Several men wearing leather jackets or vests embroidered with the Galloping Goose Motorcycle Club were resting under the shady awning to the right of the restaurant. Their club logo is golden yellow with purple embroidery and depicts a raised middle finger with "MF" written on the back of its hand. The hand is attached to a pair of booted legs running in spotty underpants. Behind this hand is an outhouse, with another hand at the front door holding a bottle with two Xs inscribed on the front. Galloping Goose is a one-percenter—i.e., outlaw—motorcycle club founded in Los Angeles in 1942. It became an official club in 1946 and established chapters in nine other states.[6]

The Galloping Goose members were resting in exactly the same spot where Jimmy and Mike catch their breath in "Bad Choice Road." We didn't get into much detail as we talked, but they were kind enough to let me photograph a few of their group and some of the bikes parked outside the burger joint. They told me to tell the FBI they were nice guys. (I haven't had reason to talk to the FBI recently, so I'm printing the message here.) They hadn't heard of the fictional Dorado Kings, a motorcycle club that hangs out at the Dog House in *Better Call Saul* season 4, episode 5, "Shotgun."

The item to order is the Laguna Burger, a half-pound certified Angus beef patty seasoned fresh and served on a locally baked brioche-style bun, with all the fixings, including Hatch green chile, iceberg lettuce, tomato, melty American cheese, pickles, mustard, and red onion. Americans are as particular about the assembly of condiments on their burgers as the English are about assembling cream and jam on a scone. Here at Laguna, it's worth noting that no sauce makes direct contact with the bun, preserving the bun's structural integrity whether you rip the wrapper off right then and there in the service station or take it in your car to eat on the road. The order on my burger from the bottom up looked like this: red onion and pickles (enough quantities of both to cover the entire base of the bottom bun), smashed patty with mustard spread on top, American cheese, green chile, tomato, lettuce, and a top bun sprinkled with sesame seeds. A red-and-white checkered greaseproof paper wrapper, with a plastic sword skewer pushed through the middle, holds the burger together, locking in all that fresh grilled flavor.

You can also order a Laguna Wimp (a third-pound Laguna Burger that still comes with all the fixings) for a smaller appetite. If you're in need of more sustenance, a Laguna Burger meal adds fresh-cut fries to the order. Either way, the burgers are "Never Frozen, Always Amazing."[7] Laguna Burger also serves a variety of hot dogs (though they vary by location), including a Corn Dog, a Frito Pie Dog, a Chile Cheese Dog, and the Classic Dog with relish, mustard, and diced onions; shakes; sandwiches, including the Roadrunner Chicken; and sides. The Chile Cheese Fries here come with red chile with ground beef, shredded cheddar, and diced onions. Route 66 Casino Hotel, just a few minutes west of the 66 Pit Stop, posted a photo on their Facebook page of actor Benicio Del Toro enjoying a Laguna Burger at their location when he was in New Mexico shooting *Sicario: Day of the Soldado* (2018).[8] The kitchen is right behind the cashier, so you have a beautiful view of your burger patty getting smashed to perfection on the grill.

Laguna Burger is owned by Laguna Development Corporation (LDC). Its website states, "Unlike privately owned businesses, LDC's income doesn't go to an individual owner, but rather its income is dedicated to the well-being of the Pueblo of Laguna."[9] The corporation also owns Dancing Eagle Casino, Route 66 Casino Hotel, the 66 Pit Stops, and the Route 66 Travel Centers. *Laguna* means "lagoon" or "small lake" in Spanish. The Laguna people have lived and farmed along the Rio San Jose in New Mexico for thousands of years. The pueblo's Spanish mission, San José de la Laguna, was constructed between 1699 and 1701, after the Pueblo Revolt of 1680, which expelled the Spanish from New Mexico until 1696.[10] The mission is located in the Laguna Pueblo historic district and is listed on the National Register of Historic Places. The church is still operational and celebrates Saint Joseph's Annual Feast Day on September 19. The 66 Pit Stop featured in *Better Call Saul* is at the Rio Puerco exit, off I-40. The Rio Puerco Valley, southeast of Chaco Canyon, is steeped in history and volcanic formations. Traditionally Navajo country, the valley in its heyday from the mid to late nineteenth century to World War II boasted four main Hispano settlements: San Luis, Cabezón, Casa Salazar, and Guadalupe.[11] Today, though, it's largely uninhabited because of prolonged drought and US government restrictions on grazing that took effect in the mid-twentieth century.[12]

Better Call Saul and *Breaking Bad* have maximized the rural offerings of New Mexico from the start. Who can forget the iconic shot of the ending of the *Breaking Bad* pilot, Walter White standing in his tighty-whities, holding a Smith & Wesson 4506 in front of the RV? In *Better Call Saul*'s "Bad Choice Road," the desert gets to play a headline act again as it punishes the two crooks with scorching heat. Far from being empty, the desert in *Breaking Bad* and *Better Call Saul* is a spellbinding place of transformation, disorientating hardship, and cruel beauty. While it is full of traditional cultures and stories, New Mexico's high desert is also the perfect stage for contemporary American myths.

Sidenote: There is a third Laguna Burger location, closer to the center of town, on Twelfth Street. To visit the building featured in *Better Call Saul*, take a short drive west on Interstate 40. Just make sure you take exit 140 to Rio Puerco; the Route 66 Casino Laguna Burger is off exit 114.

Keep it simple and go for a Laguna Burger, no substitutions. I found the half-pound patty plus garnish ample enough for lunch without any sides. Wash it down with a Pepsi from the soda fountain. If you're looking for a complete meal, I recommend ordering the Laguna Wimp plus fries. If you're hoping for something more substantial, throw an extra patty on your burger order.

HOTEL ANDALUZ $$$

a.k.a. upscale hotel in Albuquerque
125 Second St. NW, Albuquerque, 87102
(505) 242-9090
hotelandaluz.com

BCS s5.e9, "Bad Choice Road," April 13, 2020
BCS s5.e10, "Something Unforgivable," April 20, 2020

In "Bad Choice Road," Juan Bolsa's office was shot in the Martin J. Chávez Library at Hotel Andaluz (Chávez served as the twenty-sixth and twenty-eighth mayor of Albuquerque).[13] But of course, we first saw Bolsa's office in *Breaking Bad* season 3, episode 8, "I See You," when it was filmed at Hacienda Antigua Inn in Albuquerque, which is currently closed. In "Bad Choice Road," we see Bolsa take a phone call with Gus, a scene that mirrors the ominous phone call between these two back in *Breaking Bad*. (Check out *Breaking Bad* and *Better Call Saul* writer Thomas Schnauz's X feed for some excellent behind-the-scenes photos of the rig setup for the shots in "Bad Choice Road," at Hotel Andaluz, and beyond.[14])

FIGURE 78. Kim has room service at an upscale hotel (shot at Hotel Andaluz), *BCS* s5.e10, "Something Unforgivable" (2020). Courtesy of Sony Pictures Television.

FIGURE 79. Jimmy and Kim eat burgers in their hotel room, a set built by the crew featured in *BCS* s.5.e.10, "Something Unforgivable" (2020). Courtesy of Sony Television Pictures.

Hotel Andaluz's full-service restaurant, MÁS Tapas y Vino, serves cocktails and Mediterranean fare in the dining room and bar, and also offers food and drinks in six atmospheric alcoves known as casbahs in their grand lobby. We see Kim and Jimmy walk through the Hotel Andaluz lobby in "Something Unforgivable," when they leave their apartment to hide out at the hotel. In a funny layering of plots and shooting logistics, the on-screen location where Jimmy and Kim flee to safety is also used as the office location for Bolsa—the man who organized the hit on Jimmy that made them so unsafe in the first place.

The first look of the hotel in this episode is a tracking shot of the lobby's exquisite stone floors. So remember to look down when you walk in! The hotel's unique interior reads clearly on-screen, including the stained glass in the lobby. Kim and Jimmy's hotel room bears many of the hallmarks of the real hotel, such as historic photos and a muted lighting scheme. However, don't call Hotel Andaluz hoping to make a reservation for their room. It's a set.

When Jimmy tries to convince Kim to stay at the hotel, he cites a long list of amenities, but they're just scripted—the hotel doesn't actually have a heated pool, swim-up bar, hot tub, or spa. They do provide guests with access to a local gym, and they do have room service. In one scene, Kim returns from work and throws her keys on the hotel room's sideboard room while Jimmy is on the bed staring at the ceiling. It's shot much like Kim is returning home to her apartment after a day at the courthouse; perhaps she is more comfortable than she lets on with life on the road. Though Jimmy assures her their worries are over and they can head home, Kim decides they should stay and eat—they paid for the room anyway. Here's where we get a peek of the room service menu.

Kim reads out loud a lengthy description of a cheeseburger meal with an emphasis on the "truffle salt" string fries. In real life, the MÁS lunch menu also doubles as their room service menu. It features two burgers. The MÁS Signature Burger is a beef patty served inside a brioche bun, with Hatch green chile, cheddar or swiss cheese, onion, and pickle. The flavors focus on keeping it simple with an emphasis on quality ingredients. The also offer a vegetarian option, using Beyond Meat for the burger patty, and the same condiments plus bun found in the Signature Burger. In addition to burgers, MÁS offers a variety of meals for breakfast, lunch, and dinner, and the menu includes a substantial array of vegetarian options.

While Kim's ice-cream sundae bar is not on the real-life Hotel Andaluz room service menu, you can indulge in their signature chocolate lava cake with whipped cream. In season 5 of *Better Call Saul*, Kim's ice cream is a deliciously sweet contrast to the nasty plan in their conversation. Remember when Jimmy tells Kim to leave off the chocolate chip? His quip is actually a reference to season 5, episode 3, "The Guy for This," when he has to literally drop his mint chip ice-cream cone for a trip to see Lalo.

Sticking with offscreen amenities of the hotel, Ibiza deserves an honorable mention, having been frequented by cast and crew for several seasons of filming—of both *Better Call Saul* and other film and TV shows shooting in the area. Located on the hotel's top floor, Ibiza offers a lounge environment and has a patio with views of downtown below. Along with cocktails, it serves the MÁS menu.

Part of the Hilton Curio Collection, Hotel Andaluz was the fourth American hotel built by Conrad Hilton's franchise. Hilton was born in Socorro, New Mexico, about sixty miles south of Albuquerque. Opening its doors in 1939, this Hilton Hotel—as it was called at the time—was purportedly the first building in the state with air conditioning and was placed on the National Register of Historic Places in 1984.[15] Downtown Albuquerque has gone through many revisions since 1939, but the imposing scale of this hotel, located just off historic Route 66, is a reminder of the city's role in shaping the great American road trip. Conrad Hilton and his second wife, Zsa Zsa Gabor, spent the night before their wedding together at the hotel.[16]

I visited MÁS Tapas y Vino to order a burger for lunch and was fortunate enough to meet their food and wine manager at the time, who was also a background actor on movie and TV sets shooting in New Mexico. A background actor is not a member of the Screen Actors Guild acting union and is hired to perform as a nonspeaking character that does not have a first and last name. Background characters can have a description such as "policewomen" or "miscreant youth," and they often work in crowd scenes. If they get a bit more screen time, background actors are known as a featured extra—for example, they might appear as "a harried pedestrian" that the camera focuses on at the start of a street scene. *Better Call Saul* was extremely detailed about casting extras. Directors and writers handpicked all the extras for each episode, in addition to viewing in advance all the costumes they would wear. I remember one episode in season 5, when it took several hours to confirm whether a particular featured extra should wear pants or shorts.

The MÁS manager has since moved on to new pastures but she was happy to talk me about her work as a background actor on season 6 of *Better Call Saul*. Her scenes occurred outside Marion's house, in the snow in Omaha, Nebraska. Of course, in real life, the set in Albuquerque, New Mexico, was ninety degrees and sunny. In the scene, the background actor and her real-life boyfriend were dressed in full winter gear, walking through fake snow. Another background actor could be seen shoveling said fake snow with a shovel in their full winter-gear costume. Often, it's great to have additional action because that means you may get featured on-camera; however, on this hot, sunny day, they felt lucky their job was just to stroll!

Something about the moisture in the snow powder attracted an incredible number of mosquitoes. She described the crew going above and beyond to keep the extras comfortable and the mosquitoes at bay, and to finish shooting the scene. It was a satisfying and tiring shoot. The background actors' resting spot between takes was by Marion's house—the background actors had a little power nap on the stoop to keep them sustained. As is the case so often for background actors, her work didn't end up in the final cut. However, the work she did was still an important part of what builds the detail and texture of each scene in this show.

Order a MÁS Signature Burger at for a rich and satisfying homage to Kim.

NOTES

1. Gil Garduño, "Grandma's K&I Diner—Albuquerque, New Mexico," *Gil's Thrilling (and Filling) Blog*, July 16, 2022, https://www.nmgastronome.com/?p=306.
2. Dustin Rowles, "Reading Too Much Into 'Better Call Saul': Details You May Have Missed from 'Magic Man' and '50% Off,'" Uproxx, February 28, 2020, https://uproxx.com/tv/better-call-saul-easter-eggs-details-magic-man-50-percent-off-2/.
3. Patrick Hilps, "It Starts on the Page: Read 'Better Call Saul' Series Finale Script 'Saul Gone' by Peter Gould," *Deadline*, June 15, 2023, https://deadline.com/2023/06/read-better-call-saul-series-finale-script-peter-gould-it-starts-on-the-page-1235409760/.
4. Maria White, "Edward Ruscha 'Twentysix Gasoline Stations' 1963," Tate, Artist Book Summaries, May 2013, https://www.tate.org.uk/about-us/projects/transforming-artist-books/five-artist-book-summaries/edward-ruscha-twentysix-gasoline-stations-1963.
5. Wikipedia, s.v. "Twentysix Gasoline Stations," last modified May 11, 2023, 13:19, https://en.wikipedia.org/wiki/Twentysix_Gasoline_Stations.
6. One Percenter Bikers, "Galloping Goose MC (Motorcycle Club)," accessed February 9, 2024, https://onepercenterbikers.com/galloping-goose-mc-motorcycle-club/.

7. Laguna Burger, home page, accessed March 22, 2022, http://thelagunaburger.com/.

8. Route 66 Casino Hotel, "Benicio Del toro visits Route 66 Pit Stop to enjoy the World Famous Laguna Burger!," Facebook, November 29, 2016, https://www.facebook.com/rt66casino/photos/benicio-del-toro-visits-route-66-pit-stop-to-enjoy-the-world-famous-laguna-burge/10154646053060761/?paipv=0&eav=AfYa3Eo_1B3vM5Va8kQ890VF49c_wA5IJyibKqVAq5hwJN13690gdl-LOCwthSZsqas0&_rdr.

9. Laguna Development Corporation, "About LDC," accessed February 13, 2023 https://www.lagunadevcorp.com/about-ldc/.

10. National Park Service, "Mission San José de Laguna—Spanish Colonial Missions of the Southwest Travel Itinerary," updated April 15, 2016, https://www.nps.gov/subjects/travelspanishmissions/mission-san-jose-de-laguna.htm.

11. Nasario García, "Ghosts of the Río Puerco," *New Mexico Magazine*, updated December 7, 2021, https://www.newmexicomagazine.org/blog/post/ghosts-of-the-rio-puerco/.

12. García, "Ghosts of the Río Puerco."

13. Wikipedia, s.v. "Martin Chávez," last modified August 2, 2023, 08:09, https://en.wikipedia.org/wiki/Martin_Ch%C3%A1vez.

14. Thomas Schnauz, "Day 2 (pt 2) #BetterCallSaul 509," X, April 16, 2020, https://twitter.com/TomSchnauz/status/1250884811943604224.

15. Hotel Andaluz, "The Hotel Andaluz Story," accessed March 29, 2022, https://hotelandaluz.com/our-story/.

16. Jerri Clausing, "Hotel Andaluz Carries on Conrad Hilton's New Mexico Vision," July 10, 2018, *Travel Weekly*, https://www.travelweekly.com/Travel-News/Hotel-News/Hotel-Andaluz-carries-on-Conrad-Hilton-New-Mexico-vision.

EL CAMINO DINING ROOM $$

6800 Fourth St. NW, Los Ranchos de Albuquerque, 87107
(505) 344-0448
facebook.com/people/El-Camino-Dining-Room/100054370128118
Tuesday–Thursday, 7:00 a.m.–2:30 p.m.
Friday–Sunday, 7:00 a.m.–2:00 p.m.

BCS s6.e1, "Wine and Roses," April 18, 2022
BCS s6.e4, "Hit and Run," May 2, 2022
BCS s6.e5, "Black and Blue," May 9, 2022

The final season of *Better Call Saul* makes a feature of the historic neon sign outside El Camino Dining Room. *El Camino* is also the name of the Netflix spin-off movie directed by *Breaking Bad* creator Vince Gilligan and the name of the vintage Chevrolet truck Jesse Pinkman drives at the end of the movie. Suffice it to say, "the way" is a popular name in both the real Southwest and the one depicted in *Breaking Bad* and *Better Call Saul*.

El Camino Dining Room is in a small, stand-alone building surrounded by a gravel parking lot. The menu details the restaurant's history since its opening in 1950, including the fact that the building

FIGURE 80. Kim speaks with a client at El Camino Dining Room, *BCS* s6.e4, "Hit and Run" (2022). Courtesy of Sony Pictures Television.

FIGURE 81. El Camino exterior sign, 2022. Courtesy of Aimee Macpherson.

FIGURE 82. El Camino sopapillas, 2022. Courtesy of Aimee Macpherson.

is made from thick adobe bricks. New Mexico State University's guide to building adobe bricks details how native soil and water are mixed to form a mud paste. This paste is used to fill a mold, which is baked in the sun and wind. Adobe brick making is considered an art form.[1] On the other side of Fourth Street is an even larger sign for El Camino Motor Hotel, built in a similar Pueblo Revival architectural style. It is petite in comparison to today's Best Westerns or Travelodges that populate freeway off-ramps. Please don't go onto the hotel property unless you are a paying guest; the owners had to erect hand-painted signs tethered to shopping carts, plus little orange traffic cones, and put them outside the hotel to remind passersby that the hotel is not open to through traffic. You can get an excellent view of the layout from the bus stop right outside. Check out their website if you're interested in booking a place to stay: elcaminomotelnm.com/home.

Like Loyola's Family Restaurant in *Breaking Bad*, El Camino Dining Room is introduced in *Better Call Saul* at night. Just like Loyola's in real life, though, El Camino Dining Room is not open in the evening. The table used by Kim is to the left of the entrance. I sat on the right, behind the cashier's desk by the window. Opposite was a sideboard with pottery sculptures and a framed photograph of one of the restaurant's owners, Lydia Sakelaris, standing next to George W. Bush.

Looking over the menu, I was torn between the restaurant's two best sellers: the Huevos Rancheros and Lydia's Special, which involves two eggs any style, green chile stew, and fried tortillas in place of hash browns. I chose the Huevos Rancheros, a benchmark classic: two eggs over easy on corn tortillas with beans. I substituted the rice with home fries and got Christmas chile. Both chiles were mild. My green chile had an old-school white sauce spin to it, with pieces of green chile mixed into a milk-based roux. The home fries were generously sliced into rounds and gently crisped. They'd been placed on my chile right before the plate was served and were just waiting to soak it all in.

I ordered coffee, room for cream. It came in an orange C-ring mug with a little saucer and a small metal carafe for the cream. The brown mug Mike drinks from at the bar counter was not in evidence.

Lucky for you, the menu features sopapillas just like the ones Jimmy nibbles in "Wine and Roses." At El Camino Dining Room, the dough for the sopapillas starts with flour, sugar, salt, and baking powder. Warm water and two eggs are added to the mixture, then fried in canola oil rather than lard, making the side dish vegetarian friendly. What arrives is a pillow of fluffy, still-hot dough that you gently pull apart with your hands. I was very excited for my little turquoise plastic basket lined with parchment paper and filled with two sopapillas. The dough was light and unsweetened, and the basket came with a squeeze bottle of honey, the tip cut off, so I could slug a generous portion of honey into the corners of my sopapillas.

Gilbert Jr. was working the cashier's desk that day. His family owns the restaurant (Lydia is his grandmother), and he was more than happy to have a chat about his experience with the show. They now get fans of *Better Call Saul* dropping by all the time. The family were even featured as extras, along with Jesus, the restaurant's main cook.

If Loyola's is Mike's office, then El Camino serves as Kim's in her newfound role of public defender. She entertains a roster of clients and important guests in this restaurant throughout the final season of *Better Call Saul*. Kim is commanding, and maybe even a little bit scary, as she holds forth from her El Camino tabletop.

El Camino Dining Room is where Kim and Mike finally get a dialogue. Rhea Seehorn, who portrays Kim Wexler on-screen, directed the episode "Hit and Run," when these two infamous characters meet. They don't break bread, but it does look like Mike has a diner coffee mug in front of him just like he does at Loyola's. Like Mike, Kim is also on familiar terms with the waitstaff at her regular diner, and like Mike, she also has a steady relationship with diner coffee. During the next episode, "Black and Blue," a diner mug is featured with a shot of Kim's blank reflection in the black coffee, illuminated by the distinctive restaurant lighting above her.

The scene between Mike and Kim in "Hit and Run" gives us a wonderful opportunity to drink in the interior decor at El Camino. The Pueblo Revival style of the bar top, studded leatherette bar chairs, and decorative vigas on the ceiling have no trouble selling an authentic New Mexico atmosphere. The sheen on the tile floors and the decorative New Mexican trinkets that line the tables and adorn the walls work hard in the background of Kim's meetings to conjure up a sense of place and belonging. By contrast, Kim is increasingly detached from her surroundings—she is consumed by her obsession with destroying her former boss and mentor, Howard Hamlin (Patrick Fabian).

Order the Huevos Rancheros or Lydia's Special. Add an extra side of sopapillas, just like the ones Jimmy eats at the start of season 6. Drink a mug of diner coffee, black, in homage to Kim.

LIMONATA $

a.k.a. Rose Hill Café
3222 Silver Ave. SE, Albuquerque, 87106
(505) 266-0607
facebook.com/LimonataCafeNobHill
Monday, Thursday–Sunday, 8:00 a.m.–2:00 p.m.

BCS s6.e4, "Hit and Run," May 2, 2022

Silver Avenue SE in Nob Hill runs parallel to a stretch of Central Avenue punctuated by buildings noted for their historical import—from the modern style and architectural neon of the 1940s Nob Hill Business Center to the Territorial Revival style of Immanuel Presbyterian Church, recently added to National Register of Historic Places, this neighborhood calls forth the old Route 66. Limonata café is one of a small group of colorfully painted commercial buildings called the Village at Nob Hill. Opposite the café is the Fragrant Leaf, a boutique that sells gourmet loose-leaf tea. Limonata shares a little patio with a handful of other independently owned cafés at the Village. The eighteen-mile-an-hour speed limit on Silver Avenue means plenty of cyclists use the road to commute to the University

FIGURE 83. Kim checks the view from the Rose Café patio (shot at Limonata), *BCS* s6.e4, "Hit and Run" (2022). Courtesy of Sony Pictures Television.

of New Mexico main campus. It's only a four-minute bike ride away from the café.

Better Call Saul's season 6 features Limonata's charming patio for a single, memorable scene. Kim's motivation for seating Clifford Main (Ed Begley Jr.) on the patio is much less charming than the location. She wants him there so that he has a front-row seat to Jimmy's stunt in Howard's car on Silver Avenue. The slapstick comedy of Jimmy McGill drenched in fake tan and shouting at Wendy the hooker from the driver's seat of Howard's vintage Jaguar is genuinely funny, making it easier to overlook the downright sinister style of Kim and Jimmy's plot against Howard.

Kim and Clifford have little black menus for the café, which is called Rose Hill on the show, perhaps a play on Nob Hill. Clifford remarks that he's heard this place makes a "killer latte," and the two lawyers are served gourmet coffee made to order in white cups with saucers. A little rock fountain bubbles next to them.

Limonata offers a contemporary, unpretentious selection of all-day breakfast, lunch, and baked goods. The hot and cold drink selections are extensive and have some fun options, such as the Nitro Coffee and Jackalope Spicy Hot Chocolate, in addition to classics like Flat White, Cappuccino, and Italian sparkling water. Reasonably priced with an emphasis on local ingredients, this café exudes independently owned, small-town charm.

Order a latte to have it served with a cup and saucer, European style, like Kim and Clifford.

RANCHERS CLUB OF NEW MEXICO $$$

a.k.a. German bar (temporarily closed)
1901 University Blvd. NE, Albuquerque, 87102
(505) 884-2500
theranchersclubofnm.com

BCS s6.e5, "Black and Blue," May 9, 2022

The Ranchers Club, located inside the Crowne Plaza Albuquerque, is dubbed for a bar in Germany, in the episode "Black and Blue." The set decoration makes several changes (most notably hiding the rearing horse that is a feature behind the bar at this club). Here, Lalo charms Werner Ziegler's widow, Margarethe (Andrea Sooch), and then walks her back home. The following day, we see why as Lalo breaks into her home to search for intel on the Gus Fring project Werner was hired to realize.

Lalo and Margarethe sit at the Ranchers Club's wooden bar top. It looks like Margarethe has a white wine, while Lalo, masquerading as a New Mexican businessman named Ben, has a martini.

FIGURE 84. Lalo collects his martini at the German Bar (shot at the Ranchers Club of New Mexico), *BCS* s6.e5, "Black and Blue" (2022). Courtesy of Sony Pictures Television.

The bartender asks if he prefers vodka or gin, and Ben, a.k.a. Lalo, declines to make a preference, saying, "Whatever you like."

It is worth calling the Crowne Plaza hotel at the number above to check on the club's status. I spoke to the front-desk staff a couple of times and the Rancher's Club has has said a relaunch is in the works. It reopened briefly for a Thanksgiving 2023 pop-up and there is hope it will reopen for good by late 2024. For now, the interior's standout furnishings, including buttery leather chairs, embossed brass decor, glossy wood counters, and vintage leather saddles, are currently unavailable for the public to view. The Crowne Plaza, an IHG Hotels & Resorts property, is open. The hotel has two restaurants open for business: Stonestreet Grille, serving breakfast and lunch, and Cantina Lounge, serving dinner and dessert. Both are open daily and are in the $$ price range of this guide.

THE COPPER LOUNGE $$

1504 Central Ave. SE, Albuquerque, 87106
(505) 242-7490
copperloungeabq.com
Monday–Friday, 5:00 p.m.–12:00 a.m.
Saturday–Sunday, 5:00 p.m.–1:00 a.m.

BCS s6.e11, "Breaking Bad," August 1, 2022

The Copper Lounge features in a rapid-fire, black-and-white montage in the "Breaking Bad" episode of *Better Call Saul*. The actor buying all these drinks at the bar is Bob Odenkirk, dressed as Gene Takovic, but he is up to a Jimmy McGill–style con that delivers a Saul Goodman level of criminal in the punchline. Of course, only Gene's victim is getting toasted on booze. Gene himself has a nifty straw device, literally up his sleeve, to pump out the drink from his cup and store it in a baggie strapped to his tummy. It's subtle enough that the drunken man he entertains doesn't notice, but with those tight shots we get all the lavish detail of the disappearing-through-the-straw device.

You don't need to be a single man in a suit to enjoy the Copper

FIGURE 85. Gene gets to work in the Copper Lounge, BCS s6.e11, "Breaking Bad" (2022). Courtesy of Sony Pictures Television.

Lounge. The space was renovated in 2017, but a bar at this location has been in operation on and off since the 1960s.[2] Look up at the ornate ceilings, an original feature predating the renovation.

The Copper Lounge serves a wide range of cocktails and hot snacks, all served in a jazzy, gem-toned interior. It's likely you'll choose a seat on velvet-and-shag upholstery. The menu has plenty of descriptive detail and spunky quotes. From the classics menu, the 1980s espresso martini is served with vodka and an espresso shot made with beans from local gourmet vendor Zendo Coffee. Pair that with an order of fries and you have a smart little night out on your hands. Currently they offer parmesan-and-truffle-oil fries, so if you want to link it back to Kim in season 5, this is the route to take.

While the cocktail list is extensive, the food is by no means an afterthought. The menu ranges from little savory tastes to substantial meals like burgers. The bar also offers a few nonalcoholic beers like Free Wave and Run Wild from Athletic Brewing Company.

Start with a cocktail from the "Classics" section of the menu, and add a light snack to round out the fun.

NOTES

1. Extension Agricultural Agent, Quay County Extension Office, New Mexico State University, "ABCs of Making Adobe Bricks," reviewed by Thomas Dominguez, March 2011, https://pubs.nmsu.edu/_g/G521/index.html.

2. Rozanna M. Martinez, "Copper Cocktails: Reopened, Remodeled Lounge on Central Hosts Fundraiser," *Albuquerque Journal*, December 22, 2017, https://www.abqjournal.com/1109272/copper-cocktails-reopened-remodeled-lounge-on-central-hosts-fundraiser.html.

El Camino: A Breaking Bad Movie

THE OWL CAFE

$$

800 Eubank Blvd. NE, Albuquerque, 87123
(505) 291-4900
facebook.com/owlcafealbuquerque
Sunday–Saturday, 7:00 a.m.–9:00 p.m.

Although it doesn't feature in either *Breaking Bad* or *Better Call Saul*, the Owl Cafe (no accent on the "e") does feature two (three if you're counting the RV) of *Breaking Bad*'s most iconic characters in its brief appearance in *El Camino*. Walter White and Jesse Pinkman sit down at a diner booth, like we've seen them do so many times before. For the characters this is nothing too special, but in 2019 we fans were dreaming about seeing these actors reunite—and *El Camino* delivered.

The flashback scene occurs at some point during the timeline of *Breaking Bad*'s first two seasons. In a throwback to the meal at Denny's from season 4, episode 1, "Box Cutter," Jesse munches away at his chaotically loaded plate while Walt leaves his more orthodox meal untouched. It looks like Jesse chose from the buffet a selection of cheese cubes, pineapple, dried fruit, and iceberg lettuce with a single cherry tomato on top. Walt has a signature mug of coffee and what looks like a breakfast of sunny-side-up egg, bacon rashers, and hash browns, with a side of toast. They're sitting at a vinyl

FIGURE 86. The Owl Cafe interior in *El Camino* (2019). Courtesy of Sony Pictures Television.

FIGURE 87. Owl Cafe banana cream pie, 2022. Courtesy of Aimee Macpherson.

booth, framed by a window. If you are facing the cash register, that's on your right. It's two down from the booth with a neon sign in the window that reads "Special." An establishing shot gives us a glorious view of the beige 1986 Fleetwood Bounder, a.k.a. the Krystal Ship, with those unmistakable yellow and orange stripes You can see the RV through the window behind Jesse during the flashback.

There aren't many characters who can say "yeah, bitch" over a plate of pineapple and really look like they mean it. Jesse Pinkman may be the only one. In real life, the Owl Cafe doesn't have a buffet; everything is served to you by the friendly waitstaff. The wavy, pale-green gingham fabric and candy for sale on the counter were cozy touches added by the show.

The Owl Cafe has a striking exterior: the head of an owl, shaped out of adobe-style cement, sits atop a curved wall that evokes the owl's wings. The owl head and wings are lined with neon, which really makes the café pop at night. An establishment since 1986, the café has many features that you associate with American diners from the 1950s, such as the chrome coat stands attached to the end of the dining booths and a menu in a chrome frame attached to the tables. It is frequented by car enthusiasts, and when I visited there were five Porsche 911 Carreras in the lot.

The menu offers plenty of iconic American diner dishes to choose from, and it even uses the old-school phrase *blue-plate specials*. This American colloquialism refers to an inexpensive meal, at a casual restaurant or diner, that usually changes by the day. In use since diners became widespread in the early twentieth century, the phrase is often used as a throwback. Although American diners are now a symbol of abundance (e.g., Jesse's loaded plate of pineapple), diner food got its start during the Great Depression, when food was much more of a scarce resource in North America. Back then, the blue-plate special provided an affordable hot meal to those who couldn't afford the luxury of choice, or maybe didn't have a kitchen for cooking. The phrase's significance is neatly explained in this quote from Graham Greene's *Our Man in Havana* (1958):

> "Surely you know what a blue-plate is, man? They shove the whole meal at you under your nose, already dished up on your plate—roast turkey, cranberry sauce, sausages and carrots and French fried. I can't bear French fried, but there's no pick and choose with a blue-plate."
>
> "No pick and choose?"
>
> "You eat what you're given. That's democracy, man."[1]

The Owl Cafe also offers one signature dish that you absolutely must check out while you are here. Drum roll please . . . the banana cream pie. Owl Cafe waitstaff told me it's available in limited quantities and goes like lightning, so be sure to call ahead and check if it's your lucky day. It is stored in the standing refrigerator that makes a fleeting appearance in the first interior shot of the diner in *El Camino*.

Better Call Saul season 2 episode 2, "Cobbler," features pie, but it's not as simple as enjoying a slice in a diner. Daniel Wormald (criminal alias Pryce, portrayed by Mark Proksch) owns a baseball card collection that is his everything. Daniel also supplies Nacho with pharmaceutical drugs. When Nacho raids Daniel's house, Mike gets the card collection back for Daniel at a hefty price. By then, Daniel has involved the police, who are curious about this guy's setup and the sudden reappearance of his baseball cards. To throw the police off the scent, Jimmy fabricates a dramatic story about a gay lover who stole Daniel's cards out of revenge. But the police are still suspicious about the unusual hole in the wall at Daniel's house. To explain that away, Jimmy claims it was for concealing Daniel's homemade fetish videos. Enter the pie.

Jimmy goes one step further to sell the story. He invents the fetish in question, "Hoboken squat cobbler," which involves sitting on a pie in underpants and a vest. Daniel's special twist is that he eventually bursts into tears. Of course, this means Jimmy coaxes Daniel into making one of these videos so they can show it to the cops if need be, much to all our amusement, and much to Kim's horror. The extras on the season 2 DVD show the tape, which is over three minutes long! You can clearly see the cream pie on the sofa in front of Daniel. After some elaborate role play, he does indeed sit in it. Satisfied with this explanation, the police make no further inquiries. They incorrectly assume the hiding place was built out of shame and embarrassment about the fetish, not because he was stashing illegally obtained pharmaceuticals.

At the end of the episode, Jimmy and Kim are sharing a banana cream pie with a spoon, out of a box. Despite Kim's disapproval of Jimmy, she's enjoying this sweet treat that was used to get a client out of trouble. Couple that with the fact that she's wearing Jimmy's University of American Samoa sweatshirt, and all in all, I'm getting the strong impression she's not quite so disgusted as she initially let on. Peter Gould credits Bob Odenkirk with inventing the name for this made-up fetish: "He pitched the idea: 'Sex acts all have a name. Shouldn't there be a name for this thing?'"[2]

Again, I'm going to be taking a bit of liberty with the brief here. The place that baked the banana cream pies featured in this episode was called Savory Fare. At the time of writing (August 2022), they aren't open for business. However, as I mentioned earlier, the Owl Cafe does offer this unique dessert, and I was lucky enough to be able to order a slice on my visit.

The tall, creamy wedge of pie overwhelmed the small melamine plate on which it was served. Chilled to perfection, each bite of pie is entirely soft until your teeth hit the paper-thin, unsweetened crust. The pie filling is thick and heavy on the spoon. I think it would be comfortable to eat after a dental operation. Who knows how the crust stays dry under all that custard, but it does, and the result is a triumph of contrasts: thin pastry crust, real banana custard, and a mountain of semisweet whipped cream, topped with a handful of chopped walnuts.

This pie can't be frozen and stored; you can only enjoy it on the day it's made. A champion of the cream pie category, it is quite unlike other traditional American pies. It lacks the acidic tang of apple or cherry, the density and spice of pumpkin pie. Of course, all these options can be served warm with a scoop of ice cream. The banana cream pie would not survive ten minutes outside of the refrigerator on a New Mexico summer day. If you put ice cream on top of the whipped cream, it would sink. I don't think it has the architectural foundation to survive a picnic. Banana cream pie is a creature that requires a working power grid to survive. If you are going to eat a whole slice, bring some courage or an insulin pen.

For an authentic diner meal, order the blue-plate special. If you're lucky and banana cream pie is on the menu, you must order one slice. No excuses.

NOTES

1. Graham Greene, *Our Man in Havana* (1958; repr., London: Vintage, 2019), 175. Citations refer to the Vintage edition.

2. *Uproxx*, "How Bob Odenkirk Helped Inspire the Funniest Better Call Saul Scene Yet," accessed March 22, 2022, https://uproxx.com/sepinwall/how-bob-odenkirk-helped-inspire-the-funniest-better-call-saul-scene-yet/.

Funyuns and Fine Wine

Honorable Mentions of Featured Flavors in
Breaking Bad and *Better Call Saul*

Coffee

GALE BOETTICHER'S SUPERLAB COFFEE

BB s3.e6, "Sunset," April 25, 2010

On the internet, you can find Quora and Reddit posts dedicated to the ins and outs of the coffee made by the character of a certain fictitious German American chemist, Gale Boetticher (David Costabile).[1] There are even multiple YouTube tutorials showing you how to make coffee like Gale, such as "Build a *Breaking Bad* Style Vacuum Coffee Maker" and "Brew Perfect Coffee with Chemistry Equipment—DIY Siphon Brewer," plus a thread on StackExchange about whether there is any scientific basis for Gale's equipment.[2]

Chemists and coffee have a strong relationship that predates Gale, Walt, and the Sumatra beans brewed in their lab. Perhaps the most famous example is the CHEMEX coffeemaker, invented by chemist Dr. Peter Schlumbohm in 1941 and inspired by nonporous lab ware (for the uninitiated, that means glass). It's much simpler than anything shown on *Breaking Bad*, or discussed on YouTube and StackExchange, and the attractive design is featured in the permanent collection at the Museum of Modern Art in New York City.[3]

FIGURE 88. Gale makes coffee at the superlab, *BB* s3.e6, "Sunset" (2010). Courtesy of Sony Pictures Television.

FIGURE 89. Howard makes his wife a latte, *BCS* s6.e6, "Axe and Grind" (2022). Courtesy of Sony Pictures Television.

Gale's coffeemaker was constructed by the props department, and the superlab where Gale built this legendary device was a set, so there isn't really a place for you to visit for a drink of Gale's coffee. However, Albuquerque's burgeoning collection of craft coffee shops offer plenty of locations for you to purchase and enjoy a really great cup. Walt and Gale probably like the control, privacy, and convenience that comes with their lab setup (I'm thinking peeling off your hazmat suit to nip out is probably a real pain), but I don't think they'd be disappointed by what's on offer at some of the vendors now here in the Duke City.

HOWARD HAMLIN'S CAPPUCCINO

BCS s6.e6, "Axe and Grind," May 16, 2022

Lawyer Howard Hamlin does not drink coffee. He has tea in the morning. But in *BCS* season 6, we do see him make coffee for his wife, Cheryl (Sandrine Holt). Howard labors over a Breville coffee-maker, producing a huge cup of cappuccino with a peace sign in the foam. Cheryl dumps it in a to-go mug, destroying the art before she's tasted it. We're not sure exactly how things got so bad between Cheryl and Howard, but clearly some foam art isn't going to bridge the distance. We hear Howard's version of the situation when he talks with his therapist, but Cheryl keeps her views under wraps. There are two sides to every love story.

This coffeemaking scene has developed its own infamy online. The Coffee Channel on YouTube published a video about it, lasting over seven minutes, made just days after the episode aired for the first time.[4] It takes a deep dive into Howard's pour technic and the texture of the milk on-camera.

JIMMY'S TRAVEL MUG

BCS s2.e2, "Cobbler," February 21, 2016
BCS s5.e1, "Magic Man," February 23, 2020
BCS s5.e8, "Bagman," April 6, 2020
BCS s5.e9, "Bad Choice Road," April 13, 2020
BCS s6.e1, "Wine and Roses," April 18, 2022

This *Better Call Saul* mug was a constant companion throughout the show after its breakout in season 2's "Cobbler." The mug is canary yellow with black font that reads "WORLD'S BEST LAWYER," and it sports a sippy-cup-style lid that makes it hard to forget, right up until Kim dumps it in a trash can in "Wine and Roses" in season 6. It started as a funny gift from Kim to Jimmy, but it doesn't fit in the cupholder of his company car from Davis & Main, so he discards it. Kim gifts Jimmy a nearly identical mug in season 5's "Magic Man," with one key difference: before giving it to him, she painted "2nd" in red nail polish between "WORLD'S" and "BEST." It's a cheeky way to celebrate the reinstatement of his legal license.

We don't know exactly what Jimmy puts into the travel mug, but I think it's fair to assume it's mainly used for black coffee—until it saves Jimmy's life by taking a bullet for him in "Bagman" in season 5.

CUTBOW COFFEE ROASTOLOGY $

1208 Rio Grande Blvd. NW, Albuquerque, 87104
(505) 355-5563
cutbowcoffee.com
Tuesday–Sunday, 8:00 a.m.–3:00 p.m.

For a specific kind of coffee, like Gale and Walt enjoy, I'd recommend going to a coffee-oriented café where your drink is made to order. Enter the award-winning Cutbow Coffee.

The *Chicago Tribune* placed Cutbow Coffee at number twenty for its top one hundred places to eat in 2021.[5] Owner Paul Gallegos is known for "personally batch roasting over 70 million pounds for Peet's Coffee" before setting up his own place, which boasts a tasting room and coffee bar just up the road from Old Town.[6] The shop floor at Cutbow is an enjoyable place to sit. It has fishing-themed art on the walls in homage to the shop's namesake, the cutbow trout. You can drop by for a takeout order or sit and relax at one of the indoor or outdoor tables. There is a large roasting machine at the front of the store.

When I visited, jazz was playing on the speakers and an employee was next to the roasting machine neatly packaging bags of coffee beans into a row of US Postal Service boxes for online orders. It smelled amazing. Conner made me a five-minute pour-over using Sumatra beans. The coffee was terrific, with a strong flavor and a gentle aftertaste. It came in a handmade stoneware mug.

Although Gallegos was busy on the shop floor, he was kind enough to take a moment to speak with me about his coffee. I asked him what he thought of coffee foam art, like Howard's in *Better Call Saul* season 6. For Gallegos, it's a bit like gilding the lily: the art comes after good coffee. Still, at Cutbow the presentation of the cup matches the quality of the brew. The drink he recommends is a pour-over, without milk or sugar, made using one of their six single-origin coffee beans. At the time of writing, Gallegos liked the Papua New Guinea Sigri Estate Peaberry, which he described as deliciously smooth and buttery. He mentioned that Cutbow is *Breaking Bad*, *Better Call Saul*, and *El Camino* executive producer Mark Johnson's favorite place to visit for a cappuccino when he's in town.

Order a pour-over from Cutbow as a nod to Gale and Walt.

Wine

Casa Esencia, a.k.a. the bar where Gus Fring goes to enjoy a glass of wine (members only)

HOTEL ALBUQUERQUE AT OLD TOWN $$
800 Rio Grande Blvd. NW, Albuquerque, 87104
(505) 843-6300
hotelabq.com/eat_drink/casa_esencia

BCS s6.e9, "Fun and Games," July 18, 2022

Alternate business (open to general public)

THE ARTICHOKE CAFE $$$
424 Central Ave. SE, Albuquerque, 87102
(505) 243-0200
artichokecafe.com
Monday–Thursday, 4:00 p.m.–9:00 p.m.
Friday, 4:00 p.m.–10:00 p.m.
Saturday, 5:00 p.m.–10:00 p.m.

FIGURE 90. Gus has a glass of red wine at an upscale wine bar (shot at Casa Esencia), *BCS* s6.e9, "Fun and Games" (2022). Courtesy of Sony Pictures Television.

Casa Esencia is a special-event venue within Hotel Albuquerque. It's not a bar accepting walk-ins, but you can rent the whole place for a celebration or purchase a membership. It has around eight thousand square feet of space, seventeen rooms, and capacity for almost three hundred people. It was built in 1783 and put on the National Register of Historic places in 1976. It looks like a traditional hacienda with modern updates. Thick adobe walls and wooden vigas face contemporary white patio furniture and a plunge pool. While the display behind the bar was modified for the show, the unique shape of the stone bar top and period detail on the doorframes remain authentic to the location.

I'm guessing that many of you will not be renting out the entire space to re-create Gus's encounter with David the sommelier (Reed Diamond), so let's head to another local: the Artichoke Café, which has a rotating selection of high-quality wines from Europe and the New World. In the past, they did have a bottle of côte rôtie (like Gus drinks) on their wine list, the 2013 Domaine Georges Vernay Côte Rôtie Maison Rouge. While that exact wine may not be on the menu when you visit, they can steer you to something excellent from their collection for you to enjoy at the counter, just like Gus. The Artichoke Cafe is an elegant but unpretentious dining venue. Like Gus's on-screen location, there is both a sit-down restaurant and a bar area. If you visit Artichoke for dinner, they have a rotating menu of seasonal dishes, which typically includes hearty vegetarian options, market fish, and indulgent desserts.

Sit at the Artichoke bar and enjoy a fine French wine.

Cucumber Water

Shooting location (permanently closed)

DAY SPA AND NAIL
160 Juan Tabo Blvd. NE, Albuquerque, 87123
(505) 332-3102

BCS s1.e1, "Uno," February 8, 2015
BCS s1.e2, "Mijo," February 9, 2015
BCS s1.e4, "Hero," February 23, 2015
BCS s2.e1, "Switch," February 15, 2016
BCS s2.e2, "Cobbler," February 22, 2016
BCS s2.e6, "Bali Ha'i," March 21, 2016
BCS s2.e7, "Inflatable," March 28, 2016
BCS s3.e4, "Sabrosito," May 1, 2017
BCS s4.e6, "Piñata," September 10, 2018
BCS s5.e5, "Dedicado a Max," March 16, 2020
BCS s5.e6, "Wexler v. Goodman," March 23, 2020
BCS s6.e4, "Hit and Run," May 2, 2022

Alternate business (open to the public)

FIGURE 91. Jimmy drinks the cucumber water at Day Spa and Nail, *BCS* s2.e1, "Switch" (2016). Courtesy of Sony Pictures Television.

LA MICHOACANA DE PAQUIME (BUSINESS INFORMATION LISTED ON PAGE 117)

High in pantothenic acid and vitamin B6, cucumber water is associated with health and wellness. If you're out and about in Albuquerque, I suggest picking up an *agua fresca de pepino* (cucumber lime cooler). You can find one at La Michoacana de Paquime. It tastes bright and refreshing, perfect for a hot summer day.

Eileen Fogarty plays Mrs. Nguyen, owner of Day Spa and Nail in *Better Call Saul*. She delivers the immortal line "Cucumber water for customer only!" multiple times throughout the seasons, starting with "Uno." She's referring to the tall dispenser of cucumber-infused water perched on a stand on the salon floor. It's something Jimmy must pass before heading to the office he rents at the back of her store. In "Switch" in season 2, Jimmy drinks straight from the spigot, in defiance of her instructions. He is done doing the right thing, and boy does he show it. While the cucumber water may not be in every shot at Day Spa and Nail, it's hard to separate the location from this iconic beverage. Since Day Spa and Nail was featured so heavily on *Better Call Saul*, you can start to see why cucumber water looms large for show fans and crew alike. Sidenote: Cucumber water was also a fun, healthy drink for the crew, and a dispenser of cucumber water made an appearance at wrap parties.

Get your cucumber fix at La Michoacana de Paquime with an agua fresca de pepino.

Whiskey

TWO FOOLS TAVERN (BUSINESS INFORMATION LISTED ON PAGE 98) $$$

The price designation refers to the more expensive whiskeys described in the entries below. The pub offers plenty of alternatives at lower prices.

BCS s1.e6, "Five-O," March 9, 2015

Whiskey drinks are the stuff of legend in *Breaking Bad* and *Better Call Saul*. There are many articles and blogs discussing their symbolic use on the show, and how they enrich the interiority of the characters who hold, taste, and sometimes even pour a double of these real-life whiskeys.

When sampling these whiskeys in Albuquerque, I recommend heading to Two Fools Tavern. Not only was it used as a location in the *Better Call Saul* episode "Five-O," but the real-life menu has a wide range of whiskeys, which gives you plenty of choice while deliberating what to sample from the list below.

FIGURE 92. Gene makes himself a Rusty Nail with Dewar's Scotch whisky, *BCS* s1.e1, "Uno" (2015). Courtesy of Sony Pictures Television.

MACALLAN

BCS s3.e6, "Off Brand," May 15, 2017
BCS s6.e8, "Point and Shoot," July 11, 2022

A nip of Macallan Scotch whisky is the way Howard and Chuck celebrate legal wins. In *Better Call Saul*, the bottle is something of a bad omen, appearing just before both Chuck and Howard die. In season 3, Howard buys Chuck a thirty-five-year-old Macallan in an attempt to cheer him up, and to celebrate Jimmy's twelve-month suspension from practicing law.

Two Fools' menu currently has six Macallans of various ages for you to choose from. Macallan is a popular single-malt whisky from the Scottish Highlands. The color is all natural, and that's not always the case with whiskeys. Many single-malt Scotches now employ caramel food dye—E150A—to achieve a specific look.[7] In season 3, Howard brings Chuck a 1966 Macallan Scotch in a wood box. In season 6, he brings Jimmy and Kim an eighteen-year-old Macallan.

Macallan is also a favorite of James Bond. A Macallan 1962 Scotch is featured in *Skyfall* (2012). Salvia, played by Javier Bardem, offers Daniel Craig's Bond a shot glass of the stuff, neat. M (the codename for the chief of MI6 in the James Bond franchise) also drinks a slightly younger vintage in their office.[8]

To give you an idea of the kind of product we are dealing with here, at Two Fools, the Macallans go from twelve up to twenty-one years. And the twenty-one-year Scotch is currently retailing for $93.75 a pour. The Macallan twelve-year Double Cask tastes fruity, with a hint of spice. It's smooth on the throat and has a festive aroma. Buy a dram for you and a colleague, and toast to "new beginnings."

DIMPLE PINCH

BB s1.e7, "No-Rough-Stuff-Type Deal," March 9 2008
BB s5.e15, "Granite State," September 22, 2013

Walt drinks Dimple Pinch, neat. Dimple Pinch is a fifteen-year-old blended Scotch whisky from Haig, which has been in business since the seventeenth century. We first see Walt drink it at the end of season 1 with his brother-in-law, Hank. And it's still his beverage of choice all the way out in New Hampshire, for the "Granite State" episode. Both episodes were written by *Better Call Saul* showrunner Peter Gould. Dimple Pinch is modestly priced in comparison to Macallan. It tastes fruity and slightly peppery; the smell reminds me of malt.

The unique bottle with its oval shape and concave "dimple" in the center of the glass makes it easy to spot on film and TV. The drink has appeared in several shows, including on a table next to Rock Hudson in *Ice Station Zebra* (1968). This movie actually makes a few appearances throughout *Better Call Saul*. Jimmy and Kim watch it during season 2, episode 3, "Amarillo," and in season 2, episode 6, "Ba'li Hai," they con someone into writing them a check for $10,000. The check is made out to Ice Station Zebra Associates. They never cash the check.

DEWAR'S WHITE LABEL

BCS s1.e1, "Uno," February 8, 2015
BCS s6.e11, "Breaking Bad," August 1, 2022

Dewar's blended Scotch whisky is used by Gene in the first episode of *Better Call Saul*. He puts in in a tumbler with ice, then mixes it with Drambuie, adding a dash of lemon, then stirring the whole drink. Voila, we have a stiff cocktail called the Rusty Nail. Gene is extra generous with the Drambuie, the Scotch whisky liqueur, making it a very sweet drink. We get to see Gene's drink this cocktail again in season 6's "Breaking Bad"—or at least pretend to while hard at work scamming at the bar.

Dewar's White Label was created in 1899[9] and it tastes of sweet citrus. It's a popular brand often used in highballs. Two Fools offers this, along with several Chivas Regal and Johnnie Walker varieties, in their blended Scotch whisky section.

WHISTLEPIG

BB s5.e2, "Madrigal," July 22, 2012

Hank, Gomez, and George Merkert (Michael Shamus Wiles) drink

WhistlePig's FarmStock Rye bourbon whiskey out of office coffee mugs in "Madrigal," ruminating over the DEA's failure to capture Gus Fring.

WhistlePig is a relative newcomer, founded by a contestant on *The Apprentice*, Raj Bhakta. The brand now sells a variety of bourbon whiskeys. On the company website, FarmStock Rye is described as having "hints of cigar box" on the nose and crème brûlée in the palate.[10] This is a rye that's easy to enjoy and macho on flavor. Perfect for pulling out of a desk drawer to boost morale with the boys.

KNOB CREEK

BB s5.e8, "Gliding Over All," September 2, 2012
BB s5.e11, "Confessions," August 25, 2013

Hank stocks another bourbon, Knob Creek, at home. He pours it neat for himself and on the rocks for Walt in "Gliding Over All." You can see the bottle in his home bar to the right of the television when he and Marie watch Walt's phony confession later in the season, in "Confessions." It's no surprise that's the drink he goes for after watching the tape. It looks like the Knob Creek that Hank owns is straight bourbon aged nine years, not twelve years. The makers describe the taste as "rich, sweet, woody."[11]

This bourbon whiskey is packaged in a bottle with a waxy seal at the top and sans serif lettering on the label. It has a large, loving fan base, and given Hank Schrader's on-screen ordeals, impeccable credentials for providing support when the going gets tough. A far more relaxing option is to head over to the bar at Two Fools and order yourself a shot with a side of Irish Nachos.

TOWN BRANCH

BCS s6.e3, "Rock and Hard Place," April 25, 2022

At the Los Pollos Hermanos factory, Mike goes to a locker and pulls out a bottle of Town Branch Kentucky Straight Bourbon Whiskey and two small glasses. He pours a shot for himself and for Nacho, who has been sentenced to death by Gus Fring. "It'll be quick," says Mike, which I guess is pretty comforting given the circumstances.

Town Branch is distilled by Lexington Brewing & Distilling Co. in Kentucky. The company's first bourbon went on sale in 2012. The Straight Bourbon Whiskey tastes earthy and isn't overly sweet.

Head to Two Fools for a show-themed whiskey tipple.

Tequila

JUBILATION WINE AND SPIRITS $$

3512 Lomas Blvd. NE, Albuquerque, 87106
(505) 255-4044
jubilationwines.com
Sunday, 12:00 p.m.–6:00 p.m.
Monday–Saturday, 10:00 a.m.–7:00 p.m.

BB s4.e10, "Salud," September 18, 2011
BCS s2.e1, "Switch," February 15, 2016
BCS s6.e6, "Axe and Grind," May 16, 2022

Zafiro Añejo is a fictional brand of tequila that is featured in both *Breaking Bad* and *Better Call Saul*. There is even a montage dedicated to the beverage from the official YouTube page of both shows.[12] We first meet this beverage in *Breaking Bad* season 4, and it goes on to be a featured in *Better Call Saul* seasons 2, 3, 4, and finally in season 6, episode 6, "Axe and Grind," where Jimmy abandons a bottle of the tequila in a liquor shop. The scene was shot in real-life independent liquor store Jubilation Wine and Spirits. The show used the lower section of the store, where paintwork, blinds, plus a countertop

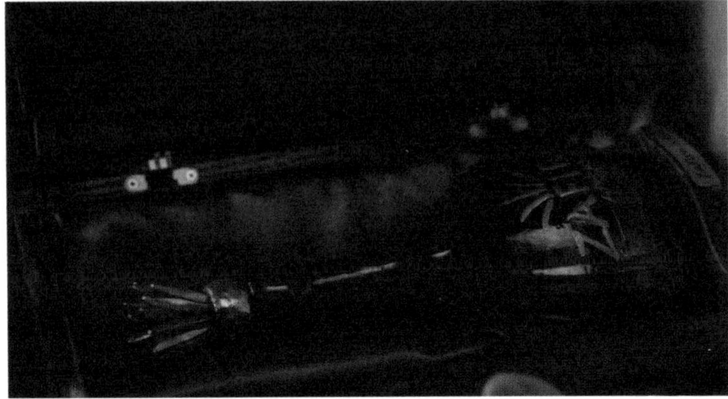

FIGURE 93. Zafiro Añejo tequila bottle, *BCS* s6.e6, "Axe and Grind" (2022). Courtesy of Sony Pictures Television.

used in the shoot are still in evidence. Jubilation itself offers many brands of tequila and mezcal, just to name a few of the beverages on offer, and their knowledgeable staff provide excellent help if you're unsure of what you'd like.

Let's take a closer look at the name of this fictional beverage. *Añejo* means "aged" or "vintage"—and what does that mean on a tequila bottle? A tequila aged between one and three years. *Zafiro* is Spanish for "sapphire," and in *Breaking Bad* is perhaps a nod to the blue color of Walter White's meth. Blue is a running theme with tequila outside the world of *Breaking Bad*: Blue agave is also the component of many quality tequilas. And there are many famous bottles of tequila that use blue in the motif. For example, the Clase Azul Tequila Reposado comes in a ceramic bottle hand-painted with blue motifs. The metal stopper has a unique-sounding ring to it when tapped against the ceramic bottle (especially when it's empty). The spirit style of the Clase Reposado (aged two to twelve months) is much younger than their Añejo.

DOS HOMBRES

I'd be remiss not to mention the aptly named Dos Hombres, the mezcal company founded by two of *Breaking Bad*'s most iconic actors, Aaron Paul and Bryan Cranston. You can enjoy a drink at many bars throughout the Duke City. Louie's Pub and Grill and Isotopes Park are two vendors that may interest show fans. The Albuquerque Isotopes baseball team played a role in the launch of this brand. As a footie fan, I have season tickets to Albuquerque's fledgling soccer team, New Mexico United (¡Somos Unidos!), who also play at Isotopes Park. A serving of Dos Hombres mezcal with a side of soda water is a refreshing beverage for the stands. I enjoyed one in a keepsake cup, which was shaped like a mason jar, complete with an orange screw-top lid. The mezcal itself is smooth and light, without the punchy, smoky taste commonly associated with many mezcals. This blend is a nice introduction to the field and is, of course, extremely quaffable.

Zafiro Añejo tequila may be the stuff of fiction, but between Jubilation's tequila selection and plenty of bars stocking Dos Hombres mezcal, you aren't far from a distilled spirit with links to *Breaking Bad*.

Ice Cream

Shooting location
Fifth St., south of Tijeras Ave., Albuquerque, 87102

BLUE BELL ICE CREAM, AVAILABLE AT WALGREENS $
3501 Lomas Blvd. NE, Albuquerque, 87106
(505) 255-8908
Sunday, 9:00 a.m.–9:00 p.m.
Monday–Friday, 7:00 a.m.–10:00 p.m.
Saturday, 8:00 a.m.–10:00 p.m.

BCS s5.e2, "50% Off," February 24, 2020
BCS s5.e3, "The Guy for This," March 2, 2020
BCS s5.e10, "Something Unforgivable," April 20, 2020
BCS s6.e13, "Saul Gone," August 15, 2022

Yes, this is a street intersection, not a restaurant or bar, but since ice cream plays a starring role here, I felt it would be wrong to omit. The end of *Better Call Saul* season 5, episode 2, "50% Off," and the start of the next episode, "The Guy for This," imbue mint chocolate chip ice cream with an aura of mystery and intrigue. If you are wonder-

FIGURE 94. Jimmy's mint chocolate chip ice cream, BCS s5.e2, "50% Off" (2020). Courtesy of Sony Pictures Television.

ing how those ants listened so carefully to direction at the start of "The Guy for This," an animal wrangler was used to help their performance. No detail is accidental on this show! In-camera effects are so important to the *Breaking Bad / Better Call Saul* universe that everything from big stunts and car wrecks to tiny little ants are rehearsed and choreographed. The ants were not filmed on location at Fifth Street, but on a stage at Albuquerque Studios. A chunk of sidewalk (and a whole lot of ice cream) was re-created for the ants' close-up. There's a fun interview in *Rolling Stone* with the wrangler, Jules Sylvester, in which he talks through the process he used for this sequence.[13] A YouTube series called "Basement Breakdown" devotes an entire episode to discuss what the *Better Call Saul* ice-cream cone means.[14] Suffice to say it's a popular moment in the show.

We can debate what the melty ice cream means until the cows come home, but I'll guide you briefly through what happens so you can make up your own mind. At the end of episode "50% Off," Jimmy is strolling down Fifth Street, ice-cream cone in hand, just minding his own business in a carefree kind of a way when a silver 1970s Oldsmobile with a maroon roof pulls up next to him. The car belongs to Blingy (KeiLyn Durrel Jones), who runs a small network of drug dealers for the Salamancas. The window goes down and Nacho beckons Jimmy, but not the ice cream, inside the vehicle. That's the kind of invitation you have to accept. So Jimmy unceremoniously dumps the ice cream on the ground as he lowers himself into Blingy's vehicle. At the start of "The Guy for This," we see an ant and then an entire ant army descend on the abandoned sweet treat melting away on the sidewalk. At its simplest, the metaphor provides us with a backstory as to why Jimmy asks Kim to leave off the mint chocolate chip ice cream when she assembles his ice-cream bowl at the hotel in season 5, episode 10, "Something Unforgivable." *Better Call Saul*'s fascination with everyday sweet treats evokes twentieth-century American fine art, in particular Wayne Thiebaud's still lifes of ice cream, pies, and cakes.

In "Saul Gone," the show's finale, we finally learn that Blue Bell is Jimmy's preferred brand of ice cream. His preference for the flavor mint chocolate chip is back. We don't see him eat any ice cream, but as Gene/Saul/Jimmy, he includes Friday deliveries of the stuff as a final and ridiculous note in his plea deal, emphasizing "no substitutions." The particularity of the request reminds me of Chuck's thing for Fuji apples. These brothers are particular.

Blue Bell Mint Chocolate Chip has a milky-green hue that really pops. But the minty flavoring from peppermint oil doesn't turn the ice cream green; that comes from artificial coloring. We don't know the exact formula, but the ingredients list on the carton includes two food dyes: Yellow 5 and Blue 1. There's also some annatto color in it too. Sugar, high-fructose corn syrup, plus vanilla extract ensure this sweet treat does not taste bitter. The chocolate chips are richer than milk but sweeter than a 70 percent cacao bar; the taste is not quite Junior Mints but it's in the neighborhood. They add a crunchy texture to the ice cream, which stops it disappearing quite so fast in your mouth. This ice cream is soothing, sugary, and absolutely refreshing on a hot day, especially when it's finished with the baked crunch of a waffle cone. Blue Bell Ice Cream is sold at Walgreens, Smith's, and Lowe's in the city of Albuquerque. I've given you the address of a Walgreens where I saw Jimmy's favorite flavor in stock most recently.

Head to Walgreens for a pint or half gallon of Blue Bell Mint Chocolate Chip: "No substitutions!"

Supermarkets

JERRY'S MARKET (INTERIOR) $

7553 Isleta Blvd. SW, Albuquerque, 87105
(505) 873-1688
facebook.com/p/Jerrys-Market-100057233838502/

HIGH-LO MARKET (EXTERIOR; PERMANENTLY CLOSED)

2515 Fourth St. NW, Albuquerque, 87102

BB s2.e3, "Bit by a Dead Bee," March 22, 2009

As vendors for lauded treats like Funyuns and Gatorade, supermarkets also feature as locations in their own right. In *Breaking Bad* and *Better Call Saul*, these food retailers are normal, routine places and their familiarity to the viewers amplify the strange or unpredictable behavior of the characters who perform there. Visit for the surreal, and purchase three bags of Funyuns while you're there.

In a kind of nightmarish striptease to the sound of Muzak, the store clerk in *Breaking Bad*'s "Bit by a Dead Bee," finds articles of Walt's clothes throughout the store before arriving at the man himself,

FIGURE 95. Marion goes shopping at Stadium Super Market, *BCS* s6.e10, "Nippy" (2022). Courtesy of Sony Pictures Television.

stark naked. This episode is another absolute national treasure from Peter Gould. Walt's dramatic way of faking a problem to cover up a real problem (in this case, staging a "fugue state" to account for the fact he disappeared a couple of days) shows a character who will go the distance to keep a secret. Marie worries if the incident was at Whole Foods (there are currently two in Albuquerque). Luckily for her, Walt decided that was not an appropriate venue for his spectacle. The blue-checkered floor tiles and blue corrugated iron walls inside Jerry's Market are a clear sign it is an independent store.

Jesse's taste for shelf-stable supermarket snacks means this is the perfect time to collect some for your own, because as he says in *Breaking Bad* season 2, episode 9, "4 Days Out," "Funyuns are awesome." Funyuns "Onion Flavored Rings" come in a bright-yellow packet with green font and a picture of the chips on the front. The Flamin' Hot edition is easily identified by a picture of acid-red Funyuns on the front of the packet. Produced by the Frito-Lay company, these are a sister chip to the Frito. Unlike Fritos, Funyuns are composed of several complex ingredients, including onion powder, garlic powder, and buttermilk (less that 2 percent of each included in the packet); it would be difficult to make one at home. That doesn't stop Funyuns from delivering on taste. They have a loud, acidic flavor that is well complemented by the airy crunch from deep-fried enriched corn meal. Their rough texture and unique "O" shape mimic a battered onion ring.

"Gatorade me, bitch" is something only Jesse could say, like he does in *Breaking Bad* season 3, episode 10, "The Fly." The question is, What flavor does he like? It's hard to mention Gatorade and *Breaking Bad* without drawing on the popular theory of which shade of blue Gatorade looks most like show's fictitious crystal meth. Common opinion falls on Glacier Freeze. It's certainly a brighter aqua than Cool Blue but less green than Frost Arctic Blitz. The ingredients include the food dye Blue 1. If the bottle is cold enough, and you're sweating enough, I think it tastes like cherry lemonade. It's hard to smell the drink, but visually the orange cap really stands out against the blue liquid inside. You can always water it down to make it last a bit longer. Gatorade was born in a lab at the University of Florida during the mid-1960s.[15] The royalties from the Gatorade Trust exceeded $1 billion in 2015.[16] It's a popular drink throughout the United States.

Pick up three large bags of Funyuns and a bottle of Glacier Freeze Gatorade for a Jesse Pinkman–themed snack.

ALBERTSONS MARKET $

11825 Lomas Blvd. NE, Albuquerque, 87112
(505) 293-9280
local.albertsonsmarket.com/nm/albuquerque/11825-lomas-blvd-ne.html
Sunday–Saturday, 6:00 a.m.–10:00 p.m.

BB s2.e1, "Seven Thirty-Seven," March 8, 2009
BB s5.e6, "Buyout," August 19, 2012

Albertsons is a supermarket chain founded in Boise, Idaho. It's extremely successful across the United States, and there are thirteen locations in or around Albuquerque.[17] In *Breaking Bad*, the chain isn't seen on-camera, but Skyler chooses prepared food from the hot bar at this chain more than once, and the chicken she offers to reheat for Walt comes from the prepared foods section of this supermarket.

In the season 5 episode "Buyout," Skyler carries into the home a large paper Albertsons grocery bag. The following meal is extremely awkward. Jesse compliments her on the green beans with slivered almonds, and she replies, "They are from the deli . . . at Albertsons." Albertsons does have a green beans almondine cold dish. Green beans almondine is a French recipe. Green beans are prepared by blanching them in hot water and then dunking them in an ice bath. They're then mixed with toasted, sliced almonds and melted butter to make the nuts stick to the beans, often garnished with grated lemon zest, garlic, and finely chopped shallot. This side is quick to prepare, crunchy, and mildly acidic.

Earlier in the series, in season 2's "Seven Thirty-Seven," Walt's experience selling meth involves witnessing Tuco beat to death

No-Doze (Cesar Garcia), a lieutenant in Tuco's northern cartel drug ring. Walt returns home, shell-shocked. Skyler makes an offhand remark that she picked up grilled chicken from Albertsons and she can heat some up for him—a particularly unappetizing offer if you've just watched someone get pounded to death, and a perfectly innocuous one if you live a normal life. Albertsons has grilled chicken breast in the Deli Side Dishes & Meals section. It also sells packs of frozen grilled chicken. Sidenote: there are currently three Albertsons in Albuquerque; the above address is just one example for you to choose from.

Shop like Skyler and head to an Albertsons for green beans almondine and grilled chicken breasts.

TRIANGLE GROCERY $

12165 NM 14 Cedar Crest, 87008
(505) 281-3030
trianglegrocery.com
Sunday–Saturday, 7:00 a.m.–8:00 p.m.

BCS s3.e8, "Slip," June 5, 2017

Now it's *Better Call Saul*'s turn to dip into the supermarket. The show used the real name of this store, Triangle Grocery. In season 3's "Slip," Chuck, feeling relatively stable, is on the hunt for soy milk. He picks up a fictitious brand called Idyllwild. Chuck is, of course, extremely particular about his shopping lists, as he demonstrates with his mild-mannered roasting of Ernesto (or Ernie, played by Brandon K. Hampton) over apples in season 1, episode 10, "Marco." Granny Smiths are a no, Fujis should be in season. Ernie was sent by Hamlin, Hamlin & McGill (HHM) law partner Howard to help Chuck. Grocery shopping isn't in his job description, but "it's a few extra bucks." Unfortunately, Chuck is too obsessed with his own problems to see past the grocery list and appreciate the humans trying to help.

STADIUM SUPER MARKET (PERMANENTLY CLOSED)

1312 Broadway Blvd. SE, Albuquerque, 87102

BCS s6.e10, "Nippy," July 25, 2022

Marion is highly skilled at using her claw grabber to remove canned goods from the shelves and place them in the front of her mobility scooter. She stops to try a cheese sample from a display at the deli counter. The cheese is called Schnauz Farms extra-sharp Wisconsin cheddar, and it is not to her liking! This brand of cheddar cheese is not one you can find at a real supermarket. It's a cheeky, loving reference to screenwriter Thomas Schnauz, who wrote and directed many episodes of both *Breaking Bad* and *Better Call Saul*. A common practice when filming in a supermarket is to swap out known brands on packaged goods to avoid copyright infringement. Set decoration replaces the known brands with packaging that is designed in-house. The logos on goods is one of the reasons why such a commonplace location can require a lot of forethought and preparation to get camera ready.

Soda

BB s1.e6, "Crazy Handful of Nothin'," March 2, 2008
BB s2.e8, "Better Call Saul," April 26, 2009
BB s3.e4, "Green Light," April 11, 2010
BB s5.e7, "Say My Name," August 26, 2012
BCS s6.e7, "Plan and Execution," May 23, 2022

Coca-Cola is shown in *Breaking Bad* as a canned beverage, as a brand on a vending machine used to conceal a gun, and as a world view. Walt's question to Declan—"Do you really want to live in a world without Coca-Cola?"—is possibly my favorite line in the show. The rhetorical question is emblematic of the *Breaking Bad* talking style, front-loaded with American popular culture references and aggressive statements. Walt explains the quality of his product is akin to "classic Coke," a nod to the descriptor "Classic" on the red Coca-Cola can. Coca-Cola added the descriptor in the 1980s so customers wouldn't confuse it with New Coke, and then dropped it in 2009. Later known as Coke II, New Coke was something of a commercial flop, and was phased out in the early 2000s. Today Coca-Cola Classic is known as Coca-Cola Original.[18] And you can enjoy it just like

FIGURE 96. Walter drinks Canada Dry Ginger Ale, *BB* s1.e6, "Crazy Handful of Nothin'" (2008). Courtesy of Sony Pictures Television.

Walt did, chilled and straight from an aluminum red can. The deep-caramel-colored soda is mildly caffeinated and tastes of a combination of flavors like vanilla and cinnamon as well as a hint of neroli and nutmeg. The Coca-Cola website does not list the nutritional value of this beverage by the 330-millileter can but by the 20-ounce bottle. This form has 57 milligrams of caffeine, and the highest ingredient after carbonated water is high-fructose corn syrup. If you're drinking it from a cup, popular additions include ice (from cube to pebble, there are many schools of thought on the best kind) and a straw (depending on the state, this may or may not be disposable). You can also marinate meat with it and use it to clean dirty coins. The red-and-white label is one of the most recognized soda logos in the world.

At the Hamlin, Hamlin & McGill law firm in *Better Call Saul*, Howard shows his kinder (or maybe obsessive?) side with Cary (Sam Song Li), who drops soda as he restocks the conference room fridge. Howard shares his twist trick to deactivate exploding bubbles in the can—not something he wants a client to experience when opening one of the dropped Schweppes Ginger Ales. Walt drinks Canada Dry Ginger Ale in "Crazy Handful of Nothin'" in season 1 of *Breaking Bad*. Critics of these two sodas agree that Schweppes has slightly less fizz than Canada Dry. The latter is also more peppery in taste. Both are quite sweet.

Blue Sky soda—whose company Blue Sky Beverage Company was founded in Santa Fe, New Mexico—is featured a few times throughout the shows. Two notable entries are in *Breaking Bad* season 2, episode 8, "Better Call Saul," and season 3, episode 4, "Green Light." The brand itself was discontinued in 2021.

BREAKING BAD AND *BETTER CALL SAUL*–THEMED GROCERY LIST

Jesse

- Funyuns
- Glacier Freeze Gatorade
- Cauliflower

Skyler

Green beans
Grilled chicken
Raisin Bran or Raisin Bran Crunch

Mike

Pistachios
Pimento cheese
Sliced white bread

Jimmy

Blue Bell Mint Chocolate Chip ice cream

Chuck

Half gallon of soy milk
Fuji apples
Bags of ice

Deputy District Attorney Bill Oakley

Fritos
Powdered donuts

Marion

Pound and a quarter of pastrami
Sumatra coffee beans
Coca-Cola
Canada Dry Ginger Ale
Schweppes Ginger Ale

Vending Machines

MISTER CAR WASH, FORMERLY OCTOPUS CAR WASH, A.K.A. A1A CAR WASH $

9516 Snow Heights Cir. NE, Albuquerque, 87112
(505) 298-8833
mistercarwash.com/store/snow-heights
Sunday, 8:00 a.m.–6:00 p.m.
Monday–Saturday, 7:30 a.m.–6:00 p.m.

BB s1.e1, "Pilot," January 20, 2008
BB s3.e11, "Abiquiu," May 30, 2010
BB s4.e2, "Thirty-Eight Snub," July 24, 2011
BB s4.e3, "Open House," July 31, 2011
BB s4.e6, "Cornered," August 21, 2011
BB s4.e7, "Problem Dog," August 28, 2011
BB s4.e9, "Bug," September 11, 2011
BB s4.e10, "Salud," September 18, 2011
BB s5.e1, "Live Free or Die," July 15, 2012
BB s5.e3, "Hazard Pay," July 29, 2012
BB s5.e7, "Say My Name," August 26, 2012

FIGURE 97. Jimmy looks at the broken courthouse coffee vending machine, *BCS* s1.e2, "Mijo" (2015). Courtesy of Sony Pictures Television.

BB s5.e9, "Blood Money," August 11, 2013
BB s5.e10, "Buried," August 18, 2013
BB s5.e11, "Confessions," August 25, 2013
BB s5.e13, "To'Hajilee," September 8, 2013
BB s5.e14, "Ozymandias," September 15, 2013

In *Breaking Bad* season 4, episode 6, "Cornered," Walt finally takes over the car wash. The previous owner, Bogdan Wolynetz (Marius Stan), walks him through the building and taunts him by questioning whether Walt is ready to be "the boss" of this business. Can he be tough enough? Clearly this rubs Walt, the millionaire meth entrepreneur, the wrong way. But he acts on his disdain for Bogdan's remarks in a very controlled fashion. He makes Bogdan leave him the framed "first dollar" from when he opened the car wash business. Without ceremony, Walt smashes open the frame to get at the dollar, walks to the vending machine in the car wash, and spends the money on a soda. It looks like it's a Coke. Bye-bye, Bogdan's sentimental memories. The same vending machine is still in place at the car wash in season 5's "Confessions," when Walt pretends to be looking at a broken latch on the machine but is actually collecting his revolver (.38 snub nose).

In *Breaking Bad*, this car wash changes hands at least twice. First Walt and Skyler purchase the business from Bogdan in "Open House" in season 4, and then A1A Car Wash is seized by the State of New Mexico in "Granite State" toward the end of season 5. Even though the real-life business changed hands in 2014, it still resonates profoundly with *Breaking Bad* fans. It's also a busy car wash frequented by locals. When I visited, a local watched his car get detailed through the glass screen. Commenting on my camera, he said he'd been getting his car washed here since the Octopus days. He was amazed that people are still visiting from all over the country, a decade later, to gawk at a car wash in Albuquerque. There is always a steady stream of *Breaking Bad* fans when he visits.

But this is a car wash, not a restaurant or bar! While that may be true, it also has something key to the *Breaking Bad* and *Better Call Saul* universe: some great vending machines. Not only are they functional and accessible to the public, but they are also stocked with show-relevant snacks, in addition to other popular beverages like ice tea and water. One sells drinks (choose Gatorade or Coca-Cola if you are sticking with the *Breaking Bad* theme) and the other sells snacks (Funyuns are in there, but alas no Fritos). Coca-Cola is a popular beverage, and to the casual observer it's nothing remarkable to see one here. But if you love *Breaking Bad*, selecting a Coke, from a vending machine, at the A1A Car wash . . . well, that's special. Unfortunately, the machine does not dispense cans. You will have to make do with a plastic bottle. But there is comfort in knowing the flavor will be the same as the stuff on-screen.

Mister Car Wash typically has free popcorn and coffee available to its customers. That's not the case at this location, or at least it wasn't when I visited. My guess is there are so many *Breaking Bad* fans wondering through that providing free popcorn to everybody would be

FIGURE 98. *BB*–themed vending machine at Mister Car Wash, 2022. Courtesy of Aimee Macpherson.

a challenge for the bottom line. Much like the Twisters on Isleta, the waiting room has *Breaking Bad* paraphernalia on the walls, some official and some homemade. There is a third vending machine (the most I've seen in one space to date), with *Breaking Bad* emblazoned on the front, that dispenses show-themed T-shirts. When I visited, there were only a couple of shirts in the machine. Headshots of the cast remain up on the walls as well as a signed photograph from the *Breaking Bad* locations department.

When I left, one staff member said "Have an A1 day" in homage to the slogan Walt and Skyler came up with. The large empty lot next to the car wash was often used as a base camp for the working trucks and trailers on *Breaking Bad* and *Better Call Saul*. Today it's mostly empty, and that makes for easy parking.

COURTHOUSE VENDING MACHINE

BCS s1.e2, "Mijo," February 9, 2015
BCS s5.e1, "Magic Man," February 23, 2020

Better Call Saul puts the vending machine center stage. The Heron of Alexandria is credited with inventing the first vending machine; it was a coin-operated Holy Water dispenser.[19] His research on automation has survived in a body of work now known as *Pneumatica*. Among many devices, he also created a lot of machinery for Greek theater. Perhaps the most famous form of Greek theater is the genre of tragedy, and perhaps the cornerstone of Greek tragedy is the concept of fate. It only seems fitting that the inexorable fate of Jimmy's path to Saul-hood, his manipulation of a broken system, is symbolized by a broken vending machine (with its origins in ancient Greece) at a courthouse spewing out hot coffee on the floor—like it does at the end of "Mijo." No one rushes into shot to clean up the mess, and the machine keeps pumping out hot java.

I can't think of a subtler or funnier way to poke fun at present-day artisan coffeehouse culture than Jimmy McGill's obsession with the coffee from the vending machine at the courthouse. Our antihero is routinely seen taking a cup of what is almost certainly terrible-tasting coffee and using it in gags, hanging around with it . . . I feel like the machine is basically a character at this point. Now I'm going to have to try to let you down gently. This coffee vending machine is a piece of set dressing, brought and removed by the crew. You can't go visit it, and here are two good reasons why: number one, it's stored away in a warehouse somewhere as property of Sony Pictures, and number two, the location where the machine is filmed is generally closed to the public. The machine is only used for scene-specific work at Bernalillo County Annex, 415 Tijeras Avenue NW, Albuquerque, 87102. The building used to be a courthouse and is still owned by the county. Currently it is home to the Administrative Services Division and Professional Standards Division of the Bernalillo County Sheriff's Office. The present-day Bernalillo County Courthouse, which houses the Second Judicial District Court, is located at 400 Lomas Boulevard NW, and the Bernalillo County Metropolitan Court is right across the street at 401 Lomas. Neither have a coffee vending machine in the building.

One of this machine's absolute knockout performances in season 2's "Mijo" features an unconventional shot style that became synonymous with *Breaking Bad* and *Better Call Saul*. (This episode was in fact directed by *Breaking Bad* producer and director Michelle MacLaren.) You know what I'm talking about here: the camera POV is facing out, "peep-o," style from an unusual or unexpected location. In "Mijo," we are looking out from inside the coffee machine as Jimmy leans down to inspect it. Finding the cup-holding device broken, Jimmy doesn't attempt to fix it but just walks away while the coffee gushes down, unable to fill the tipped-over cup. And if that isn't a metaphor for "the system is broken," I honestly don't know what is!

Now I'm going to make a momentary detour out of coffee and into food, specifically the moment with Deputy District Attorney William "Bill" Oakley (Peter Diseth) and the courthouse snack vending machine (or if you're in the biz, that's known as a "full-line" vending machine) in "Magic Man." Again we have the infamous "peep-o" camera POV, shot from within the machine itself. DDA Oakley's selection is a New Mexico favorite, Fritos. However, the Fritos get jammed in the machine just as they are about to fall into the tray. Oakley checks the hallway and since it's empty, he does the classic trick of body slamming the machine to dislodge the stuck chips.

Although he paid for the chips, the move isn't exactly aboveboard and gives as a nice little window into the mind-set of this government official. He hasn't broken bad, but the guy does behave a little differently when no one is watching. Frito chips are little curly strips made from a corn-based batter. The only other ingredients are corn oil and salt; they are gluten free. The original flavor tastes a little bit like toast with salted butter. It's enjoyed as a snack on its own but is also used as a topping on Frito pie. This chip has been popular in the United States for almost eighty years.[20]

Get your car detailed at the Snow Heights car wash. Treat yourself to a Gatorade or Coca-Cola from one of the three vending machines in the customer waiting area.

NOTES

1. Quora, "Was Gale Boetticher's Coffee Maker on Breaking Bad Real or Replicable?," accessed March 29, 2022, https://www.quora.com/Was-Gale-Boetticher-s-coffee-maker-on-Breaking-Bad-real-or-replicable; Reddit, "Help Recreating Gale Boetticher's Coffee Set Up," accessed March 29, 2022, https://www.reddit.com/r/chemistry/comments/1jr3nf/help_recreating_gale_boettichers_coffee_set_up/.

2. Jonathan Katz Moses, "Building a Breaking Bad Style Vacuum Coffee Maker," July 7, 2019, YouTube video, 13:33, https://www.youtube.com/watch?v=M5ahUyS7EEo&ab_channel=JonathanKatz-Moses; Beals Science, "Brew Perfect Coffee with Chemistry Equipment—DIY Siphone Brewer," November 8, 2018, YouTube video, 7:18, https://www.youtube.com/watch?v=mECCEQllg5Y; StackExchange, "Chemistry Behind Gale's Coffee Maker in Breaking Bad," last modified December 23, 2021, https://chemistry.stackexchange.com/questions/7439/chemistry-behind-gales-coffee-maker-in-breaking-bad.

3. CHEMEX, "History," accessed March 29, 2022, https://www.chemexcoffeemaker.com/gallery/album/history.

4. Coffee Channel, "Coffee Expert Reacts to Coffee Scene in Better Call Saul Season 6 Episode Six," May 27, 2022, YouTube video, 7:11, https://www.youtube.com/watch?v=k5XnR4yKwpE&ab_channel=TheCoffeeChannel.

5. *Chicago Tribune*, "Top Places to Eat in 2021, According to Yelp," February 19, 2021, https://www.chicagotribune.com/dining/table-talkers/sns-yelp-top-places-to-eat-2021–20210219-h324q6dhp-5foliid3hv3nvk7te-photogallery.html.

6. Cutbow Coffee Roastology, home page, accessed March 29, 2022 https://www.cutbowcoffee.com/.

7. Emily Bell, "Wait, There's Food Coloring in My Expensive Whiskey?" *VinePair*, September 29, 2015, https://vinepair.com/wine-blog/why-there-is-food-coloring-in-your-expensive-whiskey/.

8. Bond Lifestyle, "The Macallan Whisky," accessed February 9, 2024, https://www.jamesbondlifestyle.com/product/macallan-whisky.

9. Dewar's, "Dewar's White Label," accessed September 8, 2022, https://www.dewars.com/us/en/double-aged-whiskies/dewars-white-label-whisky/.

10. WhistlePig, "FarmStock Rye," accessed January 26, 2024, https://www.whistlepigwhiskey.com/whiskeys/farmstock.

11. Knob Creek, "9 Year Bourbon Whiskey," accessed February 9, 2024, https://www.knobcreek.com/our-products/ketucky-straight-bourbon-whiskey.

12. Breaking Bad & Better Call Saul, "Zafiro Añejo Tequila, Breaking Bad & Better Call Saul," August 27, 2021, YouTube video, 13:26, https://www.youtube.com/watch?v=dDfGg7LBZRc&ab_channel=BreakingBad%26BetterCallSaul.

13. Brenna Ehrlich, "'Better Call Saul': Show's Ant Wrangler Breaks Down Ice Cream Scene," *Rolling Stone*, March 9, 2020, https://www.rollingstone.com/tv/tv-news/better-call-saul-ant-wrangler-964304/.

14. Ological, "What Does the Better Call Saul Ice Cream Cone Mean? Basement Breakdown," March 12, 2020, https://www.youtube.com/watch?v=vLY9p_nL1RE&ab_channel=Ological.

15. History.com, "This Day in History: October 2, 1965," accessed September 8, 2022, https://www.history.com/this-day-in-history/gatorade-sports-drinks-inventions.

16. Darren Rovell, "Royalties for Gatorade Trust Surpass $1 Billion: 'Can't Let It Spoil Us,'" ESPN, October 1, 2015, https://www.espn.com/college-football/story/_/id/13789009/royalties-gatorade-inventors-surpass-1-billion.

17. Albertsons Market, “Find a Location,” accessed September 8, 2022, https://local.albertsonsmarket.com/search.html?q=35.0843859%2C-106.650422&storetype=5655&store-type=5655&l=en.

18. Stephanie Clifford, “Coca-Cola Deleting ‘Classic’ from the Coke Label,” *New York Times*, January 30, 2009, https://www.nytimes.com/2009/01/31/business/media/31coke.html.

19. Martyn Shuttleworth, “Heron’s Inventions,” Explorable, July 25, 2011, https://explorable.com/heron-inventions.

20. Frito-Lay, “FRITOS Original Corn Chips,” accessed March 29, 2022, https://www.fritolay.com/products/fritos-original-corn-chips.

SAMPLE ITINERARIES BY CHARACTER

THE GOOD

Hank

Blake's Lotaburger, Garduño's of Mexico, Leo's Nightclub

Jimmy

Copper Canyon Cafe, Tamaya Resort and Spa, Dog House Drive In

Kim

El Camino Dining Room, Penny's Diner, Carrie's Restaurant

THE BAD

Gus and Lydia

Twisters Burgers and Burritos, Grove Cafe & Market, Hotel Chaco

Saul and Mike

Loyola's Family Restaurant, Louie's Pub and Grill, Laguna Burger

Tuco and Nacho

Java Joe's, La Michoacana de Paquime, El Moreno Restaurante y Paleteria

Walt and Jesse

Owl Cafe, Denny's, Isleta Resort & Casino

THE UGLY

In Hiding (It's an Ugly Business)

Cinnabon, Grandma's K&I Diner, Hotel Andaluz

Scams—Albuquerque Edition

Café Lush, Limonata, Vintage 423

Scams—Chicago Edition

Edelweiss am Rio Grande, Two Fools Tavern, Bar Uno

SAMPLE ITINERARIES BY FEATURED FOOD AND DRINK

FOOD ICONS

Denny's ("Build Your Own Grand Slam" with hash browns, two orders of bacon and two sunny-side-up eggs, plus black coffee), Gino's New York Style Pizza (pepperoni pizza, unsliced), Cinnabon (Classic Roll)

DRINKS

Two Fools Tavern (Macallan Scotch whisky), Louie's Pub and Grill (Fat Tire beer), Carrie's Restaurant (Moscow Mule)

SWEET TREATS

Limonata (latte), La Michoacana de Paquime (blue bubble gum paleta), Owl Cafe (banana cream pie)

That's a Wrap

FUEL FOR THE CREW

On set, the crew are fed by the noble caterers. Snacks between meals are put together by craft service (affectionately called crafty). Every shoot day plans for an hour break, which involves a hot lunch wherever and whenever it is needed. Shoot day starts at 6:00 p.m.? Breakfast is available from 5:00 p.m. to 7:00 p.m. Shoot day starts at 6:30 a.m.? Breakfast from 5:30 a.m. to 7:30 a.m. French hours mean the crew works through lunch and peel off one department

FIGURE 99. Eggs cooking for breakfast at *BCS* catering, 2017. Courtesy of Aimee Macpherson.

FIGURE 100. Sonic to-go order for *BCS* crew, 2017. Courtesy of Aimee Macpherson.

FIGURE 101. Late-night barbecue at *BCS* production office, 2017. Courtesy of Aimee Macpherson.

at a time to collect food. This is more common in Europe than in North America, where shooting hours also tend to be shorter.

When you next watch a TV show, remember that a catering crew whipped up a specialty breakfast and lunch out of their trucks twice a day for 120 crew members (give or take) every single day of filming. If there are two locations a day, that means they prepare breakfast at one location, then move the trucks and serve lunch at the second, arriving many hours before the first meal is due. Both meals are typically served family style. You take your tray of food and eat in the "lunch box," a wide trailer filled with tables and chairs that has heating and cooling. This is a key resource during inhospitable weather (think rain or extreme heat) and rough terrain (desert scrub or a dusty parking lot). The catering trucks and lunch box take up a lot of room, so they usually have their own parking space at base camp. This is also where you find actor, costume, and makeup trailers, plus the second assistant director office truck and the better portable toilets.

Crafty are usually right by the set so the crew have access to water and nourishment (no joke when the weather is extreme and you're working outside all day). When the cameras are rolling, the crafty truck is always open. It could be providing snacks and coffee at 10:00 a.m. or 3:00 a.m. I've seen hot dogs delivered on an all-terrain vehicle over hilly desert sand, on-screen enemies piling into the crafty truck on a night shoot to share hot tea and a bite of fruit, and locally sourced sous vide eggs served up for breakfast in a downtown parking lot. These people do it all.

It may sound like the greatest luxury to someone off set, but remember that the shooting crew and actors are not expected to leave set during filming. And filming might last sixteen hours or more. The only way you are getting any water or snacks—for relief or distraction during the long shooting hours—is from crafty. Catering is the only place you can get breakfast or lunch. If you have two locations on a shooting day, the drive time between the two is scheduled into the work. That means you almost never get a chance to fold in a quick detour.

On top of that, you are often filming outside of regular business hours and/or at locations where there isn't close access to food and drink vendors—for example, freeway overpasses, windswept roads, scrapyards, downtown but it's 2:00 a.m. on a Thursday. Without crafty, or the honey wagon (that's the portable toilets), you'd get uncomfortable fast!

For the average *Breaking Bad* or *Better Call Saul* fan, it's not possible to access a film production catering meal or find a crafty truck. Here are a handful of local vendors where the crew have fueled up on over the years when they are off set or in preparation for a shoot. It's a non-exhaustive list.

BREAKFAST

Golden Pride $

5231 Central Ave. NW, Albuquerque, 87105

(505) 836-1544

goldenprideabq.com/locations

Sunday, 7:00 a.m.–9:00 p.m.

Monday–Saturday, 6:00 a.m.–9:00 p.m.

The day before shooting, a tech scout—one of the office production assistants—will call in the order. The next morning, they'll drive over to that Golden Pride location around 6:00 a.m. and collect several trays, each holding a different style, for a total of about fifty to seventy burritos, depending on crew size at the office that day. The trays were laid out in the staff kitchen at the production office, ready and waiting for the tech scout crew to grab before hopping in their bus. The tech scout crew then spend the day driving to each location featured in the episode ahead, along with that episode's director, writer, and first assistant director. On-site, the whole team works out the technical equipment required to set up the shots. Episodes are filmed back to back, so there is always a team prepping the next episode while the shooting crew is on set filming. When the shooting crew are filming the final episode, the prepping crew start to wrap up the offices, materials, and equipment that were used throughout the season. Each department has a prepping crew, so everything from wire cables to background actors' shoes can be accounted for and stored away safely in storage units owned by the studio.

Pro tip: memorize your favorite burrito number to speed up your order. Golden Pride has several locations in the city, and, FYI, their flagship dine-in restaurant, the Frontier (2400 Central Ave SE, Albuquerque, 87106), is one of the few regional fast-casual vendors to offer Coca-Cola; it goes one step further and has a Coca-Cola Freestyle machine.

If you aren't ordering breakfast for fifty, here are some other options:

Duran Central Pharmacy $
1815 Central Ave NW, 87104
(505) 247 4141
duransrx.com/diner
Monday–Friday, 9:00 a.m.–6:00 p.m.
Saturday, 9:00 a.m.–2:00 p.m.

The Farmacy $$
3718 Central Ave. SE, Albuquerque, 87108
(505) 227-0330
facebook.com/farmacyabq
Wednesday–Monday, 8:30 a.m.–2:30 p.m.

Kaufman's Coffee and Bagels $$
2500 Central Ave. SW, Ste. B900, Albuquerque, 87104
(505) 361-1734
kaufmanscoffeebagels.com
Monday, 6:30 a.m.–2:00 p.m.
Wednesday–Friday, 6:30 a.m.–2:00 p.m.
Saturday–Sunday, 8:00 a.m.–2:00 p.m.

LUNCH

Salads

Vinaigrette $$$
1828 Central Ave. SW, Albuquerque, 87104
(505) 842-5507
vinaigretteonline.com/albuquerque
Sunday–Saturday, 11:00 a.m.–9:00 p.m.

Mata G Vegetarian Kitchen $$$
116 Amherst Dr. SE, Albuquerque, 87106
(505) 266-6374
mata-g.com
Monday–Saturday, 10:00 a.m.–6:00 p.m.

Sandwiches

Curious Toast Café $$
718 Central Ave. SW, Albuquerque, 87102
(505) 737-7817
curioustoastcafe.com
Thursday–Sunday, 8:00 a.m.–2:00 p.m.

Golden Crown Panaderia $$
1103 Mountain Rd. NW, Albuquerque, 87102
(505) 243-2424
goldencrown.biz
Sunday, 10:00 a.m.–8:00 p.m.
Wednesday–Saturday, 7:00 am–8:00 p.m.

Coda Bakery $$
230 Louisiana Blvd. SE, Ste. C, Albuquerque, 87108
(505) 232-0085
codabakery.com
Sunday, 10:30 a.m.–5:00 p.m.
Monday–Saturday, 9:30 a.m.–5:30 p.m.

Hearty
Fork & Fig $$
6904 Menaul Blvd. NE, Ste. C, Albuquerque, 87110
(505) 881-5293
forkfig.com
Monday–Saturday, 11:00 a.m.–9:00 p.m.

The Shop Breakfast & Lunch $$
2933 Monte Vista Blvd. NE, Albuquerque, 87106
(505) 433-2795
theshopabq.com
Wednesday–Sunday, 8:00 a.m.–3:00 p.m.

Flying Star Cafe (local business with multiple locations around the city; the one in Nob Hill is large, and near other locations mentioned in this book) $$
3416 Central Ave. NE, Albuquerque, 87106
(505) 255-6633
flyingstarcafe.com/find-us
Sunday–Wednesday, 7:00 a.m.–9:00 p.m.
Thursday–Saturday, 7:00 a.m.–10:00 p.m.

Tacos
Barbacoa el Primo $$
1300 San Mateo Blvd. SE, Albuquerque, 87108
(505) 433-4261
facebook.com/Barbacoaelprimo505
Sunday–Saturday, 7:00 a.m.–3:00 p.m.

El Paisa $$
820 Bridge Blvd. SW, Albuquerque, 87105
(505) 452-8897
Sunday–Saturday, 8:00 a.m.–10:00 p.m.

PICK-ME-UPS WHEN YOU'RE IN THE SCOUT VAN

Zendo Coffee $
413 Second St. SW, Albuquerque, 87102
(505) 926-1636
zendocoffee.com
Sunday–Saturday, 7:00 a.m.–7:00 p.m.

Try the Turkish Latte with honey, cardamom, clove, and nutmeg. If you're looking for an ode to chemists, order a small CHEMEX. For those avoiding caffeine, Zendo has plenty of flavorful options—for example, the Sweet Bonnie with blood orange rooibos tea, vanilla syrup, and coconut milk. Once upon a time, at a set downtown, I went on a coffee run to Zendo for the rigging grip and grip crew. It was a crane shoot day, which means a big crane and lots of extra personnel. I arrived at the working truck and they handed me a list of individual orders handwritten on the back of a yardstick with a Sharpie. Zendo took the order on the stick with good grace. Every order was not only correct but also extra hot, so the crew could enjoy their off-set treat by the time I'd brought it back. Thank you, Zendo! They now have online ordering, so you can leave the yardstick on the truck.

Squeezed Juice Bar (local business with multiple locations around the city; the one on Cutler was a favorite) $$
3600 Cutler Ave. NE, Ste. 6, Albuquerque, 87110
(505) 431-0036
squeezedjuicebars.com/index.php/locations
Monday–Thursday, 11:00 a.m.–8:00 p.m.
Friday–Sunday, 11:00 a.m.–9:00 p.m.

The raw and cold-pressed juice blends from this bar are worth seeking out. The Fatigue Fighter with beet, apple, lemon, and ginger is an excellent pick-me-up. It tastes good enough to be a treat without trashing your food regime. The drinks are served in lovely glass bottles that you can return or reuse.

Sonic (a fast-food chain that currently has ten locations throughout the city; the one on Menaul is near other locations mentioned in this book) $
3800 Menaul Blvd. NE, Albuquerque, 87110
(505) 883-7041
sonicdrivein.com/locations/us/nm/albuquerque
Sunday–Thursday, 7:00 a.m.–11:00 p.m.
Friday–Saturday, 7:00 a.m.–12:00 a.m.

Sonic's signature pebble ice is available by the bag and is the fastest way to make a room temp can of soda cool down on a hot day. As a treat, sometimes the production office would pick up a couple of bags and stash them in the office freezer. They also have milkshakes—sometimes you don't need an immunity booster, and an ice-cold shake flecked with candy bar chunks is the only thing that will do!

Dairy Queen (a fast-food chain with various locations throughout the city; this location has an excellent vintage neon "Dairy Queen" sign outside) $
427 Isleta Blvd. SW, Albuquerque, 87105
(505) 877-9742
dairyqueen.com/en-us/locations/nm/albuquerque
Sunday–Saturday, 12:00 p.m.–9:00 p.m.

Order one of their signature frozen dairy drinks, and gift it to someone you truly appreciate.

DINING OUT

During the week, a crew person's workday is, at minimum, twelve hours. When Saturday rolls around, it's time to shake off work and use your per diem for something tasty. (A per diem is a small eating stipend for crew and actors who have temporarily relocated from out of state to work for a production.) Here's a small list of go-tos:

Campo at Los Poblanos
4803 Rio Grande Blvd. NW, Los Ranchos de Albuquerque, 87107 $$$
(505) 985-5000
lospoblanos.com/dining
Monday–Wednesday, 8:30 a.m.–10:30 a.m., 5:00 p.m.–9:00 p.m.
Thursday–Sunday, 8:30 a.m.–1:00 p.m., 5:00 p.m.–9:00 p.m.

Farm & Table $$$
8917 Fourth St. NW, Albuquerque, 87114
(505) 503-7124
farmandtablenm.com
Tuesday–Saturday, 5:00 p.m.–9:00 p.m.

Frenchish $$$
3509 Central Ave. NE, Albuquerque, 87106
(505) 433-5911
frenchish.co
Wednesday–Saturday, 4:30 p.m.–8:30 p.m.

La Guelaguetza Mexican Restaurant $
816 Old Coors Dr. SW, Ste. B, Albuquerque, 87121
(505) 916-0095
la-guelaguetza-mexican-restaurantllc.business.site
Sunday, 10:00 a.m.–9:00 p.m.
Monday–Friday, 11:00 a.m.–10:00 p.m.
Saturday, 10:00 a.m.–10:00 p.m.

Mesa Provisions $$
3120 Central Ave. SE, Albuquerque, 87106
(505) 494-5264
mesaprovisions.com
Wednesday–Sunday, 5:00 p.m.–9:00 p.m.

Oni $$
600 Central Ave. SW, Albuquerque, 87102
(505) 503-6722
oniabq.com
Tuesday–Thursday, 11:30 a.m.–8:00 p.m.
Friday–Saturday, 11:30 a.m.–9:00 p.m.

Salt and Board $$
115 Harvard Dr. SE, Ste. 9, Albuquerque, 87106
(505) 219-2001
saltandboard.com
Sunday–Thursday, 11:00 a.m.–9:00 p.m.
Friday–Saturday, 11:00 a.m.–10:00 p.m.

Sixty-Six Acres $$
2400 Twelfth St. NW, Albuquerque, 87104
(505) 243-2230
sixtysixacres.com
Sunday, 11:00 a.m.–8:00 p.m.
Monday–Saturday, 11:00 a.m.–9:00 p.m.

PIZZA NIGHT

Every now and then on *Better Call Saul*, actors, directors, and producers would treat the shooting crew to a pizza night. That meant Hawt Pizza would drive up to the studio and set up their wood-fired pizza oven. Yes, up that steep incline with an oven in tow! They now have a spot at the Sawmill Market, 1909 Bellamah Avenue NW, Albuquerque, 87104 (Sunday, 11:00 a.m.–8:00 p.m.; Monday–Saturday, 11:00 a.m.–9:00 p.m.). The following are also favorites:

Farina Pizzeria & Wine Bar $$
510 Central Ave. SE, Albuquerque, 87102
(505) 243-0130
farinapizzeria.com
Monday–Friday, 11:00 a.m.–9:00 p.m.
Saturday–Sunday, 4:00 p.m.–9:00 p.m.

Rumor Pizza $$
724 Mountain Rd. NW, Albuquerque, 87102
Outside seating or takeout
Online ordering only: rumorpizza.com
Wednesday–Sunday, 4:00 p.m.–9:00 p.m. a

OFF-THE-CLOCK BARS

Bow & Arrow Brewing Co. $
608 McKnight Ave., Albuquerque, 87102
(505) 247-9800
bowandarrowbrewing.com
Sunday, 12:00 p.m.–9:00 p.m.
Monday–Wednesday, 3:00 p.m.–9:00 p.m.
Thursday, 3:00 p.m.–10:00 p.m.
Friday–Saturday, 12:00 p.m.–11:00 p.m.

La Cumbre Brewing Company $
3313 Girard Blvd. NE, Albuquerque, 87107
(505) 872-0225
lacumbrebrewing.com
Sunday–Saturday, 12:00 p.m.–10:00 p.m.
Tuesday–Thursday, 12:00 p.m.–11:00 p.m.
Friday–Saturday, 12:00 p.m.–12:00 a.m.

Gravity Bound Brewing $$
816 Third St. NW, Albuquerque, 87102
(505) 308-3081
gravityboundbrewing.com
Sunday, 10:00 a.m.–9:00 p.m.
Tuesday–Thursday, 3:00 p.m.–9:00 p.m.
Friday, 2:00 p.m.–10:00 p.m.
Saturday, 12:00 p.m.–10:00 p.m.

Sidetrack Brewing Company (check out the "buy a friend a beer" board) $
413 Second St. SW, Albuquerque, 87102
(505) 800-7113
sidetracknm.com
Sunday, 1:00 p.m.–10:00 p.m.
Monday–Thursday, 3:00 p.m.–11:00 p.m.
Friday, 3:00 p.m.–12:00 a.m.
Saturday, 1:00 p.m.–12:00 a.m.

Happy Accidents $
3225 Central Ave. NE, Albuquerque, 87106
happyaccidentsbar.com
Sunday, Wednesday–Thursday, 5:00 p.m.–11:00 p.m.
Friday–Saturday, 5:00 p.m.–12:00 a.m.

DINING SUGGESTIONS FOR DIFFERENT SPEEDS

Sit Down and Savor

Breakfast at Duran Central Pharmacy, lunch at La Guelaguetza Mexican Restaurant, cocktails and dinner at Campo

Food on the Run

Breakfast at the Farmacy, lunch at the Shop, dinner from Oni

One Drink and a Light Dinner

Happy Accidents, which offers substantial snacks alongside their cocktails

ABQ STATE OF MIND

Fare Inspired by the Show Made in Albuquerque

For the reproductions to be desired,
the original has to be idolized.

—UMBERTO ECO, *FAITH IN FAKES*

BAD CANDY

The Candy Lady $

424 San Felipe NW, Albuquerque, 87104
(505) 243-6239
thecandylady.com
Sunday, Tuesday–Wednesday, 12:00 p.m.–5:00 p.m.
Monday, Thursday, 11:00 a.m.–5:00 p.m.
Friday–Saturday, 11:00 a.m.–6:00 p.m.

FIGURE 102. The Candy Lady's "bad candy," for personal use, 2022. Courtesy of Aimee Macpherson.

Albuquerque's Candy Lady is a real woman. Her name is Debbie Ball and she's been in the candy business since 1980. Debbie made the rock candy *Breaking Bad* used on-screen for their first season. Legend has it that the first batch was clear, then production asked her to add the now-famous blue color. The meth candy now sold in her store is sprayed by hand with a blue dye to get that electric hue just right. It's for sale in both a "dealer's size" and a "dime size." At the front of the shop, to the left of the entrance, is a homemade tribute to the series: A Los Pollos Hermanos logo hangs in front of the window, framed by two cardboard cutouts, one of Jesse Pinkman and the other of Walter White. In front of them are two little ornate patio chairs, painted lime green. You can sit in front of them and pose for a photograph with a tray of rock candy, a scoop, and a scale. A Jesse apron, hat, and glasses are all on standby for you to wear in the photograph if you wish. Sitting at this table gives you a view of the other half of the shop. If you look out to the right, you will see a pinboard mounted with old newspaper clippings mounted to that detail the historic escapades of the Candy Lady in Old Town.

In the eighteen-and-older section of the shop are a wide array of chocolate genitalia. These are the items that brought Debbie publicity long before *Breaking Bad* came on the scene. Available in an assortment of sizes, these chocolates are still extremely popular. Penises, breasts, and vaginas on popsicle sticks, wrapped in cellophane, are neatly stacked into colorful trays according to size (small, medium, big). The electric-pink nipples and penis tips are made in-house, just like the rock candy and multicolored fudge. Affordably priced, they are often purchased in bulk. The Candy Lady has sex and drugs covered in her store. We're all waiting to know how she'll fill out the rock 'n' roll portion of this infamous trifecta.

BETTER CALL SAL

Los Poblanos Farm Shop $$

4803 Rio Grande Blvd. NW, Los Ranchos de Albuquerque, 87107

farmshop.lospoblanos.com

(505) 938-2192

Sunday–Saturday, 9:00 a.m.–6:00 p.m.

This salt is "made with Black Italian truffle salt, fine grain salt from the Sea of Cortez and organic Sicilian oregano grown on" the Los Poblanos farm.[1] It's packaged in a very elegant little glass container. The store recommends pairing it with scrambled eggs and their Green Chile Jam on thick-cut toast. If you're looking to take home a savory homage to *Better Call Saul*, you've found "the guy for this."

BREAKING BAD BURGER

La Mexicana Tortilla Co. $
304 Coal Ave. SW, Albuquerque, 87102
(505) 242-2558
lamexicananm.com
Wednesday–Saturday, 8:00 a.m.–2:00 p.m.

The Breaking Bad Burger at La Mexicana is not a small lunch item. Two beef patties on a toasted bun come with cheese, bacon, red chile beans with meat, chile con queso, and an egg your way topped with sour cream and guacamole, with a side of french fries (crinkle cut)! The menu suggests fourteen ways to add more chile to your meal. It is currently open for takeout only, so when you order this burger, know you won't be eating it at La Mexicana. This establishment is a tortilla factory and market as well as a restaurant, so collect some house-made tortillas on your way out. Although La Mexicana does a great *Breaking Bad*–themed lunch, this eatery long predates the show. It opened in the 1930s and has been going strong ever since.

ALBUQUERQUE WORLDWIDE: REAL RESTAURANTS AND BARS OUTSIDE OF NEW MEXICO, INSPIRED BY *BREAKING BAD* AND *BETTER CALL SAUL*

An easy way to see the international devotion to Walter White and friends is by taking a quick look at the locations of fan-owned bars and restaurants. From Mexico to Saudi Arabia, Albuquerque is truly known and loved worldwide.

Break, Plaza Tec, Av. Tecnológico, 2528 63195 Tepic, Nayarit, Mexico

Breaking Bad, Ulitsa Yablochkova, 2/10, St. Petersburg, Russia 197198

Breaking Bean, 551 Cardero St., Vancouver, BC V6G 3E9, Canada

Heisenberg Haus, 164 Brisbane St., Ipswitch QLD 4305, Australia

The Lab by Heisenberg, 2540 Kin Saud Bin Abdulaziz Road, Al Andalus, Al Khobar 34437, Saudi Arabia

Los Pollos Hermanos (Las Vegas), online ordering only from Uber Eats[2]

Walter's Coffee Roastery, Caferağa, Bademalti Sk. No: 21, 34710 Kadiköy/Istanbul, Turkey

NOTES

1. Los Poblanos Farm Shop, "Better Call Sal," accessed March 29, 2022, https://farmshop.lospoblanos.com/products/better-call-sal.

2. Uber Eats, "Los Pollos Hermanos—Las Vegas," accessed March 29, 2022, https://www.ubereats.com/store/los-pollos-hermanos-las-vegas/2iYG_Ow5RUCJvu60fFxMDg?diningMode=DELIVERY.

INTERVIEWS WITH CAST AND CREW

INTERVIEW WITH TRINA SIOPY, SUPERVISING PRODUCER ON *BETTER CALL SAUL*

Trina Siopy is a producer and actress based in New Mexico. She produced *Better Call Saul* from season 5 right up to the final episode, having started on *Breaking Bad* in 2009 as an assistant property director (the property, or "props," department handles anything actors hold, eat, or drink on-camera). Trina has an incredible depth of knowledge about these shows and was an essential part of creating the world we see on these shows. Trina was kind enough to answer a few questions for me, and I hope you enjoy reading her take on food and drink in *Breaking Bad* and *Better Call Saul*!

FIGURE 103. Trina Siopy's cake pops from *BB* s5.e7, "Say My Name" (2012). Courtesy of Sony Pictures Television.

AM: As the supervising producer, you're on the shooting set almost full time. What are your favorite things to eat and drink on set to keep your energy levels up?

TS: I try to drink a ton of water, but my go-to favorite when I want a treat would have to be a cold brew with maybe a little maple syrup.

AM: Could you name one challenge with shooting food and drink on-camera?

TS: Eating food on-camera is tough on the actors and the prop crew. If actors are eating in the scene, they have to do it over and over and over again. Hopefully they like what they have to eat—not always the case. The props department has to reset the food every take and keep the food hot and edible. They also have to deal with food allergies and preferences of actors, sometimes having to make one food look like another so the actor will and can eat it.

AM: Do you have a favorite food- or drink-related prop from *Breaking Bad*?

TS: I'm kinda partial to the cake pops [featured in season 5, episode 7, "Say My Name"]. I actually made them. I remember when I first tried and was like, I can't do this. A few hours later, I had it mastered and started making the cute little piggy pops. I made a lot of the food on *Breaking Bad* 'cause I love to cook.

AM: Do you have a favorite food- or drink-related prop from *Better Call Saul*?

TS: Cucumber water for customers only!!

AM: Both shows are very location heavy. Have the real bars and restaurants of this city changed much since the start of *Breaking Bad*?

TS: Definitely things have changed. We have a lot more places opening and more variety for sure.

AM: According to IMDb, you've been a part of the *Breaking Bad* and *Better Call Saul* universe since 2009. What did you enjoy the most about working on these shows?

TS: The family that we created! The amazing writing and the pictures we painted for the world.

INTERVIEW WITH PETER DISETH, ACTOR PORTRAYING BILL OAKLEY ON BETTER CALL SAUL

AM: Oakley has several famous interactions with courthouse vending machines on *Better Call Saul*. They truly seem to have a life of their own! Could you describe how you prepared for your scenes with these machines? Did the process change season to season?

PD: After all is said and done, all I wish for Bill Oakley is that he gets one lousy win over a courthouse vending machine. His burgeoning career as a defense attorney hit some tremendous turbulence in the case of *The People v. Saul Goodman*, and who knows how that will affect him in the long run? Probably not well! So my hope is that if he can't have the big victories, maybe he can at least have a few small ones—like getting the chips or coffee he's paid for from those horrible machines. For Bill, those scenes were slow torture, just another straw on the camel's back of his patience, edging him closer and closer to just completely losing it. For Peter, though—for *me*—they were just hilarious.

FIGURE 104 Bill Oakley eats a powdered donut outside the courthouse, *BCS* s6.e13, "Saul Gone" (2022). Courtesy of Sony Pictures Television.

I loved playing those scenes at the machine because the frustration is so universal! Everyone who sees that knows what Bill is feeling, knows the small-scale tragedy of being bested by a dumb snack robot. And it says so much about Bill how he reacts every time, whether it's just giving it a dirty look or physically attacking it. He's restrained and professional, but he's also on the verge of collapse. I think it's so funny.

Preparing for those scenes was really pretty simple on my part. It was the special effects team that had the hard work! They rigged those machines—sometimes by fully tearing them apart and rebuilding them to the team's own special specifications—and operated them with remote controls. All I had to do was pop in some quarters, push a couple buttons, and know—KNOW—things are going to go my way. Because you have to believe that as an actor; you have to believe that the machine is going to work perfectly. If you're too wary of it at the top, the comedy is diminished when things go awry. The more certain he is that it'll all work out just fine, the further he falls when it doesn't.

That approach didn't change from season to season, but the given circumstances of the scene did. They had to, or else it would just be the same joke over and over. So sometimes he's just upset, other times he's full-on angry; sometimes the machine was just behaving strangely, other times the machine would full-on refuse to cooperate. We had to find variations on that moment, new ways of telling that story, for it to deserve a place in the show.

AM: Is acting with food and drink a challenge? How do you approach working with edible and drinkable props? I'm thinking of the double-chip-bag-plus-coffee lunch.

PD: Working with food and drink is one of the most challenging aspects of filmmaking for actors. In any scene, continuity (or performing the same actions in the exact same manner take after take) is so important. Aside from "oners"—sequences shot from a single camera at a single angle—each scene is generally filmed in a variety of different ways. There are master shots that show a wide view of the whole scene, there are close-ups, there are extreme-close-ups, there are over-the-shoulder shots, there are very focused inserts . . . the filmmakers get as much coverage as they can so that when the footage gets to the editors, they have a lot of material to work with in order to cut together the scene in a way that best tells the story. So if an actor performs an action, they have to try to do it the same way every time so that the different angles can fit together seamlessly in the editing booth.

This is *particularly* difficult when food is involved. It's hard to mimic taking the same bite, the same sip, the same napkin wipe take after take for hours and hours. Not to mention, if you really eat the food, you might end up having to really eat it dozens of times! I know it sounds gross, but oftentimes for these kinds of scenes, they'll have a spit bucket where an actor can "dispose of" their bites and sips between takes. But this isn't always the case!

Fortunately, most of my food scenes were just with chips and I only had to eat one or two per take, so that didn't bother me too much. I was scared when we filmed season 3, episode 3, "Sunk Costs," because I had to eat a whole bunch of french fries after already eating from my two bags of chips on the courthouse bench. It was good luck, then, that since Bob Odenkirk and I came in so prepared for our scene, we were able to film most of it in a oner, so we didn't need to do it a million times from a thousand different angles.

Unfortunately, this was not the case for the finale, "Saul Gone," when I had to eat a powdered donut on-camera. The whole gag of that moment was that Bill pops a donut into his mouth right as his phone rings, so he has to chew it up as fast as he can and swallow it down before he can answer. Which means, of course, that I didn't get the spit bucket. I ended up eating about two dozen of those things in the course of ninety-ish minutes, and let me tell you . . . that hurt! I still eat powdered donuts, but man oh man, it took me a while before I could enjoy them again!

AM: Shoot days can be long. What do you like to eat or drink on set to maintain energy levels?

PD: The challenge on set isn't to find enough food and drink to maintain my energy levels, it's to try *not* to eat *everything*. Between giant gourmet lunches, midday snacks (which are less snacks and more like full entrées—hamburgers, tacos, hot dogs, lettuce wraps, kebabs, etc., etc., etc.), and constant access to craft service carts that feature any kind of snacky item you can think of, you can do some real damage to your system!

So for me, it came down to choosing the healthiest options (protein bars, fresh fruit, and veggies), not snacking all the time, and staying hydrated with plenty of water.

But let me tell you, if you have a sweet tooth, film sets are basically heaven on earth.

AM: Oakley drinks plenty of vending machine coffee. Peter, if you drink coffee, where would you recommend for a real cup of joe in Albuquerque?

PD: I do drink coffee! I drink so much coffee! I drink *too* much coffee! In all seriousness, I do drink far more coffee than is probably healthy for a forty-year-old whose idea of exercise is to reminisce about how awful two-a-day football practices were in high school. Let's call it "remote exercise." And I know I should cut back on the caffeine . . . but so far I haven't—which I suppose is to the benefit of local coffee shops!

Every week or so, I get together with a couple other local film/TV actors and we go get real cups of joe to talk shop, agonize over auditions, gossip about the biz, share recipes and gardening tips—all that exciting stuff. We've been to several different places, but our current favorites are Zendo and Remedy Coffee [1816 Lomas Blvd. NW, Ste.

A, next to Duran Central Pharmacy]. One of us has a dog, and these two joints in particular have great outdoor seating, so we're partial to them. But we're always looking for new favorite spots!

AM: You've been a part of the *Better Call Saul* universe since season 1, episode 2, right up to the show finale. What did you enjoy the most about working on this show?

PD: This is a difficult question, not because there was so little to enjoy, but the exact opposite: everything about the experience of working on six seasons of *Better Call Saul* was an absolute joy. The work itself was challenging and rewarding, the atmosphere on set (and base camp, and the hair and makeup trailers, and the wardrobe office, and and and) was dynamic and warm, the food was incredible (yes, even the stuff I ate on-camera was tasty), and the opportunity to learn filmmaking from the best in the business was exciting and priceless. That sounds like a safe answer, doesn't it? That sounds like the "right answer." But it's also the honest one!

If I *had* to pick exactly one aspect of the experience that I appreciate over the others (oof), I suppose I would say the personal connections I made with the people there. It was like being a member of a supportive, compassionate, inspirational family. Everyone constantly raised each other up. We pushed each other to be better, but not in a way that creates tension or resentment. Rather, we pushed each other with love and trust and the steadfast belief that we could all make each other better. What a group! What an honor to have been among them!

WORKING ON TELEVISION IN ALBUQUERQUE

I was lucky enough to work on four seasons of *Better Call Saul.* I moved to Albuquerque in 2014, and once my green card came through, I got a job as a production assistant on a Tina Fey movie called *Whiskey Tango Foxtrot* (2016), which filmed in Albuquerque, Santa Fe, and in between. The working title was "Four-Ten-Four," a joke about your attractiveness on location in the army. I spent a lot of time on I-25 shuttling paperwork, ammo, and humidifiers between Albuquerque and Santa Fe at strange times of the day, in all weathers. Film jobs don't operate nine to five, so by the time shooting had wrapped, even on days where we shot in Albuquerque, I hadn't spent much time acquainting myself with my new town. I'd spent it at locations relevant to the film: at the De Anza Motor Lodge filled with sand and donkeys, the Rail Yards done up as a souk complete with fresh flowers and real fruit, and the production office, located in a disused military building in Albuquerque's International District (nicknamed "the war zone") that shared a gated compound with a K-9 training center. Occasionally as I was loading snacks into the scout van, my hands numb from packing in the chipped ice, I would see Albuquerque Police Department officers in bite suits waddling over to the training center, an obedient muzzled German shepherd on a leash guiding them to the door.

My second job in America was working for producer Robin Sweet. She hired me as her assistant for *Better Call Saul* season 2, and I worked for her on seasons 3 and 4. I was lucky to get hired the first time, and it was a dream come true to get rehired for the following seasons! Cut to 2019 and *Better Call Saul* season 5, and I was working as an assistant to executive producer Melissa Bernstein. I was pregnant at the time, and I left the show just a week shy of my due date, which turned out to be prudent because my baby arrived early. On my last day, we were filming in the desert scrub behind the studios. It was early July and hot. The snake wrangler caught a baby rattlesnake and put it in a plastic bucket. I got to see the little baby, safely, up close. "Mom is out there somewhere," mused the wrangler, adding, "Littles bite the hardest because they haven't learned how to stop." The office kindly gave me a cake (Berry Chantilly Cake from Whole Foods) and decorated my desk with balloons. I left after dark, handing in my studio badge and driving too fast down "snake road" (technically the southern end of University Boulevard, but it got its nickname from the two giant rattlesnake stone sculptures in the median) probably for the last time, full of my all-time favorite "second meal" on the job: the tofu Buddha Bowl with brown rice from Flying Star.

At that moment, I became an outsider to the shooting crew for the first time in over three years. It was also my first time "off set" since moving to America. I realized my knowledge of Albuquerque was acquired through the filter of *Breaking Bad* and *Better Call Saul*. I'd gotten to know the bars and restaurants through location scouting or wrap parties. Because so much of the show is filmed on location, I'd become familiar with areas unfamiliar to even seasoned Albuquerque locals. Yet the mainstream part of the city was still new to me.

Learning to know a city through filming means experiencing it in a completely different way than a tourist or even a resident who works regular business hours. You spend time in scrapyards and parking lots, navigating the freeway after dark and before the sun is up. You are at work before most coffee shops open and home after restaurants close. There is no such thing as bad weather, only bad clothes.

When I started to learn the city for a second time, as a new parent, it caused me to reflect on the difference between the bars and restaurants as they were perceived by Albuquerque locals and the cultish status those places held for the legions of committed fans online. When the University of New Mexico Press approached me about writing this book, I realized this is my shot at marrying the two. It's a way for Albuquerque locals to enjoy the pop culture value of their mom-and-pop cafés, and a way for the online fans to get an appetite for the real city.

Architectural critic Reyner Banham, considering architecture in Los Angeles during the early 1970s, wrote, "Between such unthinking hostility from outsiders, and equally unthinking indifference from the Angeleno . . . Los Angeles does not get the attention it deserves—it gets attention, but it's like the attention that Sodom and Gomorrah have received, primarily a reflection of other peoples' bad consciences."[1] Substitute Albuquerque for LA and the quote delivers an accurate description of the attention Albuquerque receives in popular culture today. My hope is that this book does a little to change the nature of that attention, from hostility or indifference to respect and enthusiasm.

NOTE

1. Reyner Banham, *The Architecture of Four Ecologies* (Los Angeles: Pelican Books, 1973), 235.

ACKNOWLEDGMENTS

Thank you, Sonia Dickey at the University of New Mexico Press. Thank you, Jason Strykowski and Candolin Cook, for your practical and thoughtful editorial notes.

Thank you, Robin Sweet, for giving me a job on *Better Call Saul*. Thank you, Melissa Bernstein, for hiring me also. Thank you, Trina Siopy and Peter Diseth, for contributing to this book in your own words. I'm so grateful for your time. Thank you to legendary location manager Christian Diaz de Bedoya. Obviously, nothing could be done without the genius of Vince Gilligan and Peter Gould. I'll forever value the chance I got to be a member of your crew. Thank you to my family in the United Kingdom and United States, specifically Walker. You're the best.

Walt: No chili powder.
Jesse: No, no, chili p is my signature!
Walt: Not anymore.

—*BREAKING BAD* S1.1, "PILOT"

This is a glossary of terms found in this book and commonly used in New Mexico cuisine, printed on North American casual dining menus, and/or spoken among television crews shooting in North America.

agua fresca. Spanish for "cold water," aguas frescas in New Mexico are cold, fresh drinks featuring peeled fruit, rice, or seeds blended with water and sugar. They are usually held in large clear plastic containers with lids. The drink of choice is ladled into a polystyrene cup holding ice and a disposable straw.

biscochito. The New Mexico state cookie since 1989 is spiced with cinnamon, sugar, and star anise. It's often made with lard and is popular at Christmastime. The spelling is New Mexican. It can be also be spelled *bizcochito* (not to be confused with *bizcocho*, a Spanish word for various pastries, cakes, and cookies).

burrito. Warmed savory fillings placed on a warmed flour tortilla, then rolled into a cylinder with the ends are closed on either side. In New Mexico, a burrito can be plated and then smothered with chile or wrapped in tinfoil and handheld. The flour tortillas used are generally ten inches in diameter laid flat. The girth of a rolled burrito varies greatly depending on the quantity of the filling inside. Popular fillings include spiced meats, pinto beans, and various salsas.

breakfast burrito. A burrito (see above) eaten for breakfast. Popular fillings are scrambled eggs, bacon or sausage, cheddar or jack cheese, and pinto beans plus chile (red or green).

chimichanga. A deep-fried burrito.

calabacitas. Cubed or diced summer squash sautéed in a frying pan with butter and vegetable oil. Sweet corn, onion, tomato, and green chile are common additions.

carne adovada. Chunks of pork sautéed with New Mexican chile powder and other seasonings. It can be used as filling in many savory dishes. Some examples include tamales, burritos, and enchiladas. This spelling is New Mexican—you might recognize this dish in its alternative spelling, *carne adobada*. In Mexico, guajillo or chipotle chiles are often used to marinate pork meat for adobada dishes. Carne adobada is commonly used as a filling in tacos.

chicharróns. Deep fried pig skin, often seasoned with red chile powder. It can be served inside a burrito or on the side of a main dish.

chilaquiles (*rojos or verdes*). Corn tortillas cut into wedges or strips, fried, then sautéed in salsa roja or verde. Often served with two eggs any style, common toppings include cilantro, shredded cheese, diced onion, avocado, and lime.

chile. For hundreds of years, this capsicum pepper has been cultivated and grown in New Mexico (note the state-specific spelling, with an "e"). The level of spice depends on the harvest, but the taste is often described as smoky and sweet, with a slow burn.

chile powder. Finely ground powder made from dried, deseeded, and destemmed New Mexican chile pods. The chiles are dried by hanging them off a string in large, longish bunches (ristras). A loop at the top of the ristra lets the chiles hang outside in the sun. They dry into a deep red color, wrinkled and brittle to the touch. Ristras of drying chiles are often used as decor. Red chile powder is used to make red chile sauce or stew, and ranges in color from earthy orange to brick or crimson.

chile relleno. Whole fresh New Mexico chiles are roasted, peeled, then delicately cut on one side in order to deseed the chile while preserving its shape. Once deseeded, the chile is stuffed with a cheese-based sauce. The cheese is often shredded jack or asadero. The stuffed chile is coated in flour and an egg white batter, then fried in a pan of hot oil.

fresh chiles. These peppers can be green or combine various shades of red and green on one pepper. They are on the large side, anywhere between four and seven inches long.

Red, green, or Christmas? This is an abbreviation of the question "Which sauce would you like to add to your savory dish?" Your options are red chile sauce, green chile sauce, or a combination of the two. The exact ingredients of the sauce will vary restaurant to restaurant, so do ask if it the sauce is vegetarian or gluten free.

roasted chiles. Whole fresh peppers roasted in a steel mesh drum turned over an open flame. Cooled roasted chiles are peeled and deseeded by hand. They are slippery to the touch and are the color of fresh chile peppers once the charred skins are removed. Peeled and deseeded roasted chile are commonly used as garnish on a burger patty or chopped and mixed into sauce or stew.

chili. Ground beef sautéed in chili powder. The chili powder is made from an assortment of capsicum peppers and other spices, such as oregano, paprika, or cumin. This means there is a sliding scale of heat to the dish, depending on the ground chilis used. Two common varieties of chili are Southern and Texan.

enchiladas, stacked New Mexican style. Whole corn tortillas fried in a pan, drained from the oil by resting on a paper towel, then layered with diced white onion, chile sauce, and shredded cheese (commonly cheddar or jack). The stack of two or more tortillas is smothered in chile sauce, red or green, though red is popular with this dish. It is sometimes topped with more shredded cheese, then broiled. Sometimes blue corn tortillas are used in place of yellow corn.

flauta. A large corn tortilla filled with shredded spiced meat (commonly beef or chicken), then rolled tight into a cigar shape and deep fried.

Frito pie. Chili con carne poured over Frito corn chips is a dish associated with Tex-Mex cuisine (Frito corn chips originated in Texas), but the dish has subtle variations across the Southwest. In New Mexico, Frito pie can be served with either chili con carne or chile sauce (red, green, or Christmas). It is often served in a Frito chip bag that is partially sliced down the middle. Common garnishes include shredded cheese, diced raw onion, shredded lettuce, diced tomato, and avocado.

Hatch. A small village in Doña Ana County, New Mexico. New Mexican chile peppers grown in the area are well known and are identified on menus as "Hatch chile." This village calls itself the chile capital of the world.

hot dog. This fast-food snack is a sausage link served in a specialty bun with garnish. It is not made with dog meat—the name refers to the shape of the sausage link because it resembles a dachshund. Frankfurters, or wieners, are the sausage type used and they come in a variety of lengths. The meat is usually pork but can also be beef, chicken, or turkey. Occasionally, the sausage combines several meats. The sausage is steamed or grilled, then placed in the bun. A hot dog bun is soft, and partially cut along the side. Its unique shape is long and thin enough to encase most of the sausage. Sometimes the bun is lightly toasted before the sausage is placed inside. Classic garnishes include mustard and diced onion. There are plenty of regional differences across the United States.

> **chili dog.** This refers to a hot dog garnished with chili, onion, and cheese. They can be up to a foot in length, otherwise known as a foot-long dog. The chili is typically shorthand for chili con carne, a beef stew made with spices and kidney beans popular in Tex-Mex cuisine.
>
> **corn dog.** A hot dog sausage stuck onto a wooden skewer, covered in corn batter, then deep fried. The corn batter is often sweetened with sugar.

huevos rancheros, New Mexican style. A breakfast or brunch classic in New Mexico, this dish layers warm corn tortillas, refried beans, fried eggs with a runny yolk, and red chile sauce, topped with shredded cheese, cilantro or green onions, and maybe some diced avocado.

Jarritos. A Mexican brand of soft drink in a wide variety of sweet flavors.

michelada. A cocktail made with beer and tomato juice. It's often served in a glass rimmed with Tajín, a chili lime seasoning. It can have a food-based garnish like shrimp or celery, and common additions are Tabasco sauce, lime juice, cubed ice, and a straw.

paleta. A Mexican style of ice pop, paletas are commonly made with fresh fruit and water. Cream-based paletas use cow or goat milk. It's not uncommon to see flavors like tamarind, spicy jalapeño, or corn. They are often displayed stacked in clear plastic wrappers, frozen onto an oval wood stick. Sometimes they are displayed unwrapped, the wood handle sticking up. When you purchase the paleta unwrapped, they are covered with a loose plastic wrapper before being placed on the counter.

papitas. A side dish of diced potatoes (cut to a quarter inch thick) sautéed in a skillet with vegetable oil, onion (or onion powder), salt, and pepper. While cooking, the dish is briefly covered with a pan lid. It's a popular side on dinner plates.

piñon coffee. Coffee beans roasted with New Mexican piñon nuts create this naturally flavored coffee. The arabica bean is commonly used in the coffee part of this drink. Historically, piñon (pine) nuts were harvested by foragers in northern New Mexico. Piñon coffee has a distinctive taste, which many describe as sweet and buttery. New Mexico Piñon Coffee company owner Jim Franco created this southwestern coffee flavor in the back of a '52 Chevy pickup with his dog, Decaf.[1]

posole. Popular at Christmastime, this stew includes hominy, red chile powder, and slow-roasted pork or chicken. It is a deep red color. Popular toppings include lime, radish, and cilantro. Vegetarian alternatives usually swap out meat for pinto beans and vegetable broth. The Mexican spelling, *pozole*, is less common in New Mexico. There are three varieties of Mexican pozole classified by color: red, green, and white. It is closely related to menudo soup, made with tripe.

refried beans. Cooked pinto beans, fried in oil or lard, then mashed. They are usually made in advance and reheated according to the specifications of the dish.

salsa. The Spanish word *salsa* translates to "sauce" in English. I explain because many visitors from out of state sometimes confuse these salsas with red or green chile sauce. For example, a Californian may say they want "green sauce" on their burrito. To a New Mexican, that means green chile sauce, but to a Californian that probably means "salsa verde."

> **salsa roja.** A cold sauce made using red tomatoes. It is red in color and usually spicy. You scoop it up with corn chips.
>
> **salsa verde, or tomatillo salsa.** A cold sauce made using tomatillos, or Mexican husk tomatoes. They look like small, unripe tomatoes. The sauce is green in color and usually spicy. You scoop it up with corn chips.

smothered. This common adjective on New Mexican menus describes how a food item will be covered in sauce, typically in a savory context. For example, a burrito "smothered" in red or green chile means that almost the entire burrito will have the sauce of your choice poured over it.

sopapilla. A square-shaped, unsweetened puffy pastry served hot. Usually, it comes in a little plastic basket with a squeezy bottle of honey. The tip of the bottle is snipped off so that plenty of honey can be squeezed into one of the four corners of a sopapilla. This pastry often accompanies a main meal. There are two common ways to eat it in New Mexico: either rip off a corner and fill it with honey, or rip off a corner and stuff it with the contents of your meal.

> **sopapilla masa.** The dough out of which a sopapilla is made. It consists of flour, baking powder, salt, and shortening. Canola oil or lard can be used as shortening. The masa is left to stand for a short time, rolled out, cut into square pockets, then deep fried in oil until puffy and golden. It's drained and served hot.

taco. A round tortilla with filling inside it, then folded in half by hand and eaten straight away. They are commonly between five and eight inches in diameter. Tortilla varieties include corn, blue corn, or flour.

hard-shell tacos. Tacos made with corn tortillas that are fried, then folded in half to make an open clam shape. The texture is crunchy, and the hard shape makes it easy to keep the filling inside the taco. Some soft tortillas are layered in twos before the filling is added, which also helps keep the filling inside.

tamale. Made from a corn masa with a savory filling, served warm in a corn husk. Popular fillings include calabacitas, carne adovada, and green chile chicken stew. They can be steamed straight from the freezer and are popular at Christmastime.

torta. A cold white-flour bun or roll with a warm, meaty filling such as carnitas, which is pork braised in lard on a low heat until it is tender, then lightly fried. Another classic filling is beef barbacoa, a mix of chuck roast, brisket, and beef cheeks slow cooked until juicy and soft. Each cook has their own version, but the meat is marinated in a seasoning that generally includes a combination of dried guajillo and ancho chile peppers, plus Mexican oregano.

NORTH AMERICAN CASUAL DINING MENUS

biscuits. A bread roll, leavened with baking powder, that is typically served warm. Biscuits can be savory or sweet.

blue-plate special. An inexpensive warm meal without substitutions; ingredients change often to keep the meal affordable.

breakfast sandwich. A sandwich served at breakfast time. Typically, fillings include fried or scrambled egg, cheese, and bacon. The bread can be toast, bagel, or even a croissant.

chicken tenders. White meat from a chicken that is breaded, seasoned (usually with onion and garlic powder, plus add-ons like dried parsley, paprika, or lemon pepper), and then deep fried. They are mass-produced and are typically longer and thinner than the oval chicken nugget. Tenders are commonly served with fries and a dipping sauce like ketchup.

club sandwich. A cold sandwich that often includes lunch meat, iceberg lettuce, tomato, and mayonnaise. It's typically presented cut into triangles, stacked, and held together with toothpick.

coffee. In the context of a North American diner, this means coffee made in a drip filter and served from a warmed glass pot that can hold several cups of coffee. It is not made to order; you cannot specify the bean or strength of the brew. The grounds are often "from the packet." It is inexpensive and usually refills are free, otherwise known as a "bottomless cup."

coffee creamer. Shelf-stable liquid or powder added to coffee. Creamers are often dairy free, using artificial sweetener and oil to create a texture that mimics real cream. It comes in many flavor—for example, Italian cream cake, hazelnut, or pumpkin spice.

cream. In the context of a diner, this can refer to light cream, which is between 18 and 30 percent butterfat; half-and-half, which is light cream and milk; or "long-life milk," an ultra-high-temperature-treated milk often available on the diner table in a 12-millileter container next to packets of sugar and sweetener.

dinner plate. Often abbreviated to "plate," it indicates that extra food is included in the meal, not just the food item listed under the meal's description on the menu. For example, "enchilada plate" might mean the enchiladas come with rice and beans plus a sopapilla on the side. Even though it is called a dinner plate, it is often available at brunch or lunchtime. It does not refer to the material or style of plate on which the meal is served.

family style. Food presented on large platters from which you serve yourself, rather than individual portions served on individual plates.

fountain drinks. Soda from a self-service drink dispenser as opposed to a sealed can or bottle.

French vanilla ice cream. The base for this ice cream is made with eggs. American vanilla ice cream means the ice-cream base is not made with eggs. Vanilla beans or vanilla extract can be used to flavor both styles.

french fries. Thin strips of potato (typically russet) deep fried in vegetable oil, typically yellow in color.

curly fries. Potatoes cut with a spiralizer, then deep fried and seasoned with paprika, onion powder, garlic powder, and salt; typically orange in color.

from scratch. When the components of the meal are made fresh to order, without using ingredients prepared in advance.

gravy. Juices from cooked meat thickened with wheat flour and/or cornstarch to make an opaque white sauce. There are many varieties.

hash. Chopped meat, cubed potatoes, and sliced onions sautéed in a frying pan.

hash browns. Shredded potatoes fried until golden brown.

home fries. Cubed potatoes parboiled, seasoned, then sautéed in a frying pan.

ice-cream float. Soda served in a tall glass with a scoop of ice cream.

> **float.** This can be an abbreviation of ice-cream float or a type of bottled soda aimed at replicating the taste of an ice-cream float.

melt. A sandwich featuring melted cheese (typically American or jack).

milkshake, or shake. Milk, ice cream, plus flavorings are pulverized in a blender and then served in a tall glass with a straw. Common toppings include whipped cream and a maraschino cherry.

> **hand dipped.** Ice cream from a container is scooped by hand and put into the blender.
>
> **malt.** A milkshake made with malted milk powder.

on the side. When a food item is served on its own plate next to the main meal or shares a plate with the main meal but isn't on the main product. For example, mustard can be put on the side of the plate rather than inside the burger bun.

pie à la mode. Translated from the French, *à la mode* means "in fashion." This dish consists of warm fruit pie topped with cold ice cream. The ice-cream flavor is typically vanilla. You can find this popular desert on menus throughout North America. Although it is described in French, it is not a common dessert in France.

potato chips. Potato sliced thin and deep fried. Crunchy and served room temperature, potato chips are seasoned in a variety of flavors. "Plain chips" are seasoned with sea salt.

sundae. Ice cream served with a sauce and at least one solid topping—for example, vanilla ice cream with chocolate sauce and peanuts. Historically, it was served in a tulip-shaped glass with a very long spoon. Common additions include canned whipped cream and a maraschino cherry.

sweetener. Artificial or natural (like stevia) sugar substitutes available in small paper sachets. A single one-gram packet of sweetener is equivalent to two teaspoons of sugar.

tater tots. "Tater Tots" is a proper name trademarked by Ore-Ida company, but it is often used as a generic term on menus for grated potato shaped into small balls and deep fried.

TELEVISION CREW LINGO

base camp. A location close to set where actors' trailers, costumes, and caterers are stationed.

call sheet. A piece of paper that tells each department what time they are required to be at set and what time the camera is expected to roll. It also details what scenes will be shot, the actors involved, and the addresses of crew parking, base camp, and set. On the back is a map detailing how to get from the production office to crew parking that day. It is printed on white US legal-size paper (8.5 x 14 inches). If any changes are made, it is reprinted on pink legal paper. It is issued at wrap the day before. When the crew break for lunch, a prelim call sheet is issued, giving the crew a preview of what will likely be the schedule for the next day. It is printed on yellow paper so you don't confuse it with the final product. These days, it is also emailed as a pdf to the crew, but the unit production manager is still required to sign off on a hard copy.

call time. The time the crew are required to be at set. Usually, this is an hour before the camera is expected to roll ("shooting call"). Crew and cast involved in makeup and hair often have a call time that is several hours before the general crew call, often referred to as precall (early call).

crew parking. A location near set where the crew park their cars. They then catch a lift in a designated minivan to base camp or set. The minivan is driven by a teamster.

craft service. The department responsible for beverages and refreshments on set for cast and crew.

> **crafty run.** An errand to obtain food or drink for crew or cast.
> **crafty truck.** A truck trailer that stores food and drink purchased on the crafty run. It is usually custom outfitted with a stovetop, microwave, prep station, and a couple of refrigerators—one for beverages and another for food.

honey wagon. Portable toilet.

> **four banger.** A honey wagon with four cubicles.

film set. The location being filmed that day.

first meal. The first meal break in a working day.

first team. Principal actors and crew members required to be on set while the camera is rolling (some examples include the director, cinematographer, first assistant director, and sound boom operator).

French hours, or walking meal. This refers to when the cast and/or crew work through the first meal break. Each department breaks away one at a time to collect a hot meal from catering.

grace. When "calling grace" goes out over the walkie-talkies, via the assistant director department, that means the shooting crew have agreed to work twelve more minutes even though they are supposed to break for the scheduled first meal.

lunch box. A large trailer set up at base camp. Inside, it has tables, chairs, and heating or cooling systems. It is for the shooting crew so they can sit down to eat their lunch.

martini shot. The penultimate shot of the working day.

meal penalty. Financial compensation for the union shooting crew when the production does not break for first meal on time after the grace period.

NDB (nondeductible break). A fifteen-minute break to get a simple snack for cast and crew who have arrived earlier than the general call time.

petty cash. A small amount of production money used to make purchases for the production. For example, you would use petty cash on a crafty run.

production office. Typically, this is a fixed location where the production, accounting, and construction departments are located.

It's also where you are likely to find the prepping crews for art, set decoration, props, locations, transport, rigging grip and electric, and costumes.

rigging crew. Crew members that set up technical aspects of a set in the days before the shooting crew arrives. Typically, this is two departments—rigging electric and rigging grip. Rigging electric crew members ("riggers") lay down the cable for lights. Rigging grip will set up any equipment required to support the camera crew. These crews also disassemble equipment on set the days after the shooting crew have left.

second meal. Six hours after the cast and crew have returned to set from lunch break, they are required a second meal. This is served by the crafty team, not the caterers. Technically, they are required to have a thirty-minute break at the same time. This meal is typically warm and very close to set, not at base camp.

second team. Examples of crew members who belong to "second team" are stand-ins for the actors and the second assistant director. Second team are called in after first team have blocked the scene, while crew light the set before filming.

10–1. Walkie-talkie code for taking a bathroom break to pee. You can guess what 10–2 refers to—it indicates you need more time.

wrap. The time when filming is over for the day. It's time to wrap up the equipment and go home.

wrap party. A party for the crew hosted by the production company at the end of filming the project. It's usually held in the city where filming took place and must happen before crew members from out of state leave for home.

NOTE

1. New Mexico Piñon Coffee, "Who We Are," accessed Feb 9, 2024, https://nmpinoncoffee.com/pages/who-we-are.

SUGGESTED READING

Banham, Reyner. *The Architecture of Four Ecologies*. Los Angeles: Pelican Books, 1973.

Barthes, Roland. *Mythologies: The Complete Edition, in a New Translation*. Translated by Richard Howard and Annette Lavers. New York: Hill and Wang, 2012.

Baudrillard, Jean. *America*. London: Verso, 2010.

Cline, Lynn. *The Maverick Cookbook: Iconic Recipes and Tales from New Mexico*. Santa Fe: Leaf Storm Press, 2015.

Dyer, Geoff. *Introduction: Space and the Spirit of Fiction*. London: Verso, 2010.

Fandom. Breaking Bad Wiki. Updated January 5, 2024. https://breakingbad.fandom.com/wiki/Breaking_Bad_Wiki.

Greene, Graham. *Our Man in Havana*. 1958. Reprint, London: Vintage, 2019.

Ruscha, Edward. *Twentysix Gasoline Stations*. Los Angeles: National Excelsior Press, 1963.

Valdez, Mark P. *A Guidebook to Breaking Bad Film Locations*. 4th ed. Self-published, CreateSpace, 2017.

Wenders, Wim. *Written in the West, Revisited*. New York: Distributed Art Publishers, 2015.

LOCATIONS BY REAL MEALTIMES

This list does not include bars and restaurants that are currently closed. Some venues are open for breakfast, lunch, and dinner, or cocktails and dinner. I've listed these businesses in the category they open first. For example, Denny's is open twenty-four hours a day, seven days a week; I've put this restaurant in the Breakfast & Lunch category since that is the first available meal of the day.

BREAKFAST & LUNCH

LUNCH & DINNER

SMALL BITES

BARS

LOCATIONS BY APPEARANCE IN BOTH *BREAKING BAD* AND *BETTER CALL SAUL*

With the list below, you can look up bars and restaurants featured in both shows. Since *Better Call Saul* is a prequel to *Breaking Bad*, the sets in *Better Call Saul* tell a story *on-camera* that predates *Breaking Bad*. In real life, the *Better Call Saul* sets were built after *Breaking Bad*. Scenes shot at these locations were often filmed years apart. The exterior of Saul Goodman's office was a location for over a decade, from 2009 to 2022. The interior of Twisters, the main Los Pollos Hermanos restaurant, was first shot in 2009, and appeared last on our screens in 2020. From 2012 to 2017, it wasn't featured.

In practical terms, the art and set decoration departments performed a unique kind of restoration project on these locations to deliver on-screen continuity. Many of these locations are living businesses, which naturally change their appearance over time. The exterior views seen out their windows are also subject to change. For example, the Albuquerque Rapid Transit bus stop near Loyola's was completed in 2017. Re-creating the look from *Breaking Bad* for *Better Call Saul* is not as simple as unwrapping a set from storage. At the opposite end of this spectrum, some locations look virtually unchanged. Louie's Pub and Grill today, for example, looks almost the same as it first appeared on-screen in 2011.

From redesigning room layouts to rebuilding upholstery, from employing graphics to conjuring ways to obscure changes to the interior and exterior of a business, the work involved in prepping these locations was extensive and often started months before a camera was scheduled to arrive. Much work also went into building a full picture of how these locations were used in previous episodes. The art department would build a file that contained all sorts of visual details—for example, where characters sat, what they sat on and what color it was, previous notable shots or angles that captured a scene, and floor plans. This enabled the episode director to understand the visual history of a location within the show. In a location that has a component built onstage, these visual notes were key to enabling storytelling continuity. Stage builds like the interiors of Gus Fring's office, Saul Goodman's office at the nail salon, Kim's apartment, and the superlab had to link to entryways on location. Once these entryways were established in an episode, the same entryways had to be used in all the episodes afterward to maintain the illusion that location and stage set were the same place.

The Bourbon House 23
Burt's Tiki Lounge 17
Dog House Drive In 5
Gino's New York Style Pizza 44
Louie's Pub and Grill 60
Loyola's Family Restaurant 63
Savoy Bar & Grill 19
Twisters Burgers and Burritos 28